HAPPINESS SOLVED

HAPPINESS SOLVED

Climbing One Hundred Steps

SANDEE SGARLATA

ARCHWAY
PUBLISHING

This book is a work of non-fiction. Unless otherwise noted, the author
and the publisher make no explicit guarantees as to the accuracy of
the information contained in this book and in some cases, names of
people and places have been altered to protect their privacy.

Archway Publishing books may be ordered
through booksellers or by contacting:

Archway Publishing
1663 Liberty Drive
Bloomington, IN 47403
www.archwaypublishing.com
844-669-3957

Because of the dynamic nature of the Internet, any web addresses or
links contained in this book may have changed since publication and
may no longer be valid. The views expressed in this work are solely those
of the author and do not necessarily reflect the views of the publisher,
and the publisher hereby disclaims any responsibility for them.

Any people depicted in stock imagery provided by Getty Images are
models, and such images are being used for illustrative purposes only.
Certain stock imagery © Getty Images.

ISBN: 978-1-4808-9702-1 (sc)
ISBN: 978-1-4808-9700-7 (hc)
ISBN: 978-1-4808-9701-4 (e)

Library of Congress Control Number: 2020918931

Print information available on the last page.

Archway Publishing rev. date: 1/26/2021

To one of my dearest friends, Trish Kapinos. Trish has an abundance of love and light, and I was able to write this book because of her influence in my life to always keep learning, searching, and growing. I cannot imagine getting this far in my life without her love and support.

This book is also dedicated to God, my team of angels, my spirit guides, and my loved ones on the other side who have been giving me miracles and signs to fulfill my life's purpose. Thank you for not giving up on me. I am eternally grateful for your continued guidance, love, and support.

FOREWORD

In the chiaroscuro of today's society, and in such times where there seems to be little light, it's important that there be those who shine a little brighter than the rest. Sandee Sgarlata is one such person.

I think we all can at least agree on this: The riddle of life is that we all-too-often encounter hurdles, challenges, obstacles, jerks, tragedies, brick walls, and despots.

In my TEDx Talk in 2013, I talked about the importance of being alive and taking creative risks. When confronted with tragedy, to echo the words of a good friend of mine, "Life isn't fair, but God is good." Or as I say in my talk, "Life isn't fair, but the world sure is beautiful." Translation: happiness is possible. And that's what Sandee's book is about.

From her time as an incredibly successful figure skating coach to her work as a corporate executive, and in her personal as well as professional life, Sandee inspires. Upon much prompting, she has recollected the stories of people returning to her years later, thanking her for impacting them so much. And this book will allow her to bring to you, the reader, this same impact.

My only advice is read this book as if it's your own life. Realize that it is about you, and your journey. When life throws a curveball, a lemon, a brick wall … happiness is still within reach. The joy of your childhood is still within reach.

Sandee and I share elephants in common. That's a long story. But let me keep this piece of writing brief, and quote a little bit of the poet Hafiz to close.

To paraphrase Hafiz's great poem "Elephant Wondering", there's a seed that has sprouted under a leaf in a forest. The seed is understandably worried about the "moseying habits of the elephant."

"Why?" asks the poet?

"Because in this lucid, wine-drenched tale, the elephant is really God, who has his big foot upon us."

Stick with me here...

Hafiz's elephant's foot is now on the yellow leaf, and the little seed is sprouted underneath, scared to be crushed. Well, the seed in that poem is the "sprouting universe, wherein we are all a little concerned and nervous."

But if you know anything about elephants, it's that they have big feet, but they tread quietly. (I learned that from my business partner, Randy Baker, who came across a quiet herd of elephants once.)

Sandee's book, and her life's work, is all about helping us with this problem of the (metaphorical) gentle elephant, the leaf, and the sprouting seed. And about solving happiness.

Part practical and part poetry, read this, and change your life in incremental yet substantial ways. Then, you will be happier tomorrow than you are today, possibly as happy as you ever have been, and quite possibly even as happy as you ever can be.

— Dr. Kent Gustavson
Prize-winning writer, TEDx speaker,
& co-founder of Thought Leader Path
www.thoughtleaderpath.com

ACKNOWLEDGMENTS

I want to take this opportunity to thank the people in my life who have my back, no matter what.

My mother: You have been my best friend and the one person I know I can always count on. You have inspired me to be the person I am today, and I can't imagine my life without you.

My siblings, Debbie, Denny, Randy, and Joe: we have endured so much together, and I love you all more than you will ever know.

Dr. Sonja: I am so grateful to have had you as my best friend for thirty-two years and counting. You are always my biggest cheerleader and know what to say to help me get through anything.

Karen D.: You have been there for me more than anyone else and I am so grateful for our friendship. I can always count on you when I need it the most and I love you for that!

My other close friends, Michele B., Lisa L., Sonja K., and Aznive K.: you are all there for me when I need it most, and I am grateful for your friendship and love.

My "girls," Deanna, Julie, and Natalie: my life is enriched because you three love me just the way I am.

My friends who took the time to give me constructive and amazing feedback on this book: I love you all and value our friendship: Dr. Sonja, Michele B., Karen D., Jim P., Paula D., Yolanda L., Amanda O., and April C.

Dr. Kent Gustavson and Randy Baker: I am so grateful

for your guidance, wisdom, and encouragement that have inspired me to create a movement.

My step-daughters, Brianna and Brittany: I watched you both go through an extremely difficult and life-altering experience and I am so proud of how you handled it with grace and amazing strength. I love you both!

My dear husband Brian, who continues to be my rock: thank you for your friendship, support, and unconditional love. You helped me heal my heart and I love you more than you will ever know.

Lastly, my son, Brandon: thank you for being the light and love of my life, keeping me on my toes, always giving me a hug, and telling me you love me in front of your friends. I am so proud of you, and you have taught me more than anyone else in the twenty plus years we have been together.

PREFACE

It was a sweltering hot and humid day on August 14, 2019, which was typical for East Coast weather. My husband and I were driving to Louisville, Kentucky, to move my one and only son to college. We drove through a storm, and as I sat in the passenger seat, I watched this one drop of rain that was stuck on the window. It could have been something else, though. The sun was now directly in front of us, and my vision was strained. Rain had accumulated on the edge of the car window, and tiny dots of water were moving toward the singular dot, being pulled by the gravity of the car driving 75 miles per hour. Some would pass it completely and move across the window, while others would merge with the tiny dot, increasing its size. Then it would break apart again. The process repeated itself over and over.

I was mesmerized watching all the little drops of water make their way across the window. I thought to myself, did they know what they were doing? Were they aware that in any second they would be thrown into the wind, never to have any more purpose? Suddenly, the tiny dot vanished, and all traces of rain were long gone. I could see a smudge on the window, providing evidence of the particle that had been there collecting the drops of water. It had been struggling to hold on; trying to save itself, yet eventually, its life was over. It was the natural course of its existence. Its life was here and gone in an instant.

That's how life is. Here and gone in an instant. It passes by us so quickly, literally in the blink of an eye. For me, it feels as if my son was just born yesterday. Yet, he is now a freshman in college. In a split second, he was in college, starting a new chapter of his life, as am I. You may be thinking, "What does this have to do with happiness?" By the time you are finished with this book, you will understand why I started with this story.

Please note: There is a difference between depression and feeling unhappy. If you believe you are experiencing depression, please seek the advice of a trained professional. Depression is a real and sometimes serious condition. While this book can help everyone feel better, the advice and tools discussed are not in any way meant to treat depression.

CONTENTS

CHAPTER 1

INTRODUCTION

I started writing this book in 2014 and ended up putting it aside as my life became increasingly busy. After getting my son settled at the University of Louisville in August of 2019, it was as if the flood gates opened up, and I began working on this book every chance I had. I finished the manuscript in early January 2020. Little did I know what the world would be facing in the months that followed.

I spent two more months editing the book, over and over. I am always striving for excellence, and I finally realized it was time to start the process of publishing the manuscript. I sent the manuscript to my publisher at the beginning of April 2020.

At that time, the world was still coming to grips with our "new normal" due to COVID-19. I have been working from home since March 12, 2020, and I am extremely grateful that my job is one that can be done remotely, as it is with the majority of my company's employees. I am also grateful to spend so much quality time with my son, not to mention that I have gained two extra hours in my day by not commuting to work!

However, I wake up every day in shock, shaking my head and realizing that our lives, the way the world operates, and the way people interact will be forever changed until a vaccine is available for every single human on the planet. Even then, I suspect the world will be bracing itself for the next pandemic since we have all lived through World War III with this single invisible enemy.

I have chosen not to change the manuscript due to the current circumstances. Even though everyone's lives have been impacted, some worse than others, the underlying message I am presenting is the same.

I was a competitive figure skater during my youth, and my only goal in life was to travel with the Ice Capades after graduating from high school. This was in the early 1980s, and their show was very small at that time. I auditioned during my senior year of high school, and I made it! I was beyond thrilled. Two weeks after my high school graduation, I received a letter from the Ice Capades congratulating me and informing me that I had been placed on a waiting list. For the first time in my life, I thought that maybe I should go to college since that's what most of my friends were doing.

Since I had never even considered college up to that point, I saw a fashion institute advertised in the back of a magazine and decided to apply. I ended up attending the school for one semester and did not have a good experience. I decided to come home and started working full-time. Over the next few years, I worked and took a class or two at the local community college. I loved working, and all the secretarial classes I took in high school led me to become a pretty decent legal secretary in Washington, DC. I moved out of my parents' home at the age of nineteen and roomed with a few of my high school girlfriends. By the age of twenty, I had my own apartment in Washington.

I have worked in many different industries in administrative roles, owned an information technology recruiting company, became a US national and international figure skating coach, certified life coach, public speaker, two-time award-winning author, and now, once again, recruiter. I eventually did complete my bachelor's degree, albeit thirty-five years after graduating from high school. It became more of a personal goal than a professional one. I will share more of my story throughout the pages of this book.

Happiness Solved is a book that has evolved from over thirty years of my quest to be happy. I am not a psychologist, nor do I have a degree in psychology. My degree is in business management, with a certificate in human resources management. I am a student of life who has lived over fifty years with her share of major highs and major lows. I am sharing what I have learned because my sole purpose in life is to help other people. It is actually my soul's purpose.

At the time of this writing, I work full-time in a job that is fulfilling for me, as it lets me help people find a job and offer career advice. I am in my second marriage to a wonderful man who is my best friend and whom I love dearly. I have an amazing son, who is the light and love of my life. I have two beautiful and successful step-daughters, whom I love and adore. I take care of my mother, who lives in a senior living community, and for that, I am incredibly grateful. I have a lot of close family and friends and a busy social life.

Before I go on my short rant below, please understand that nothing in this book is meant to make you feel bad about yourself in any way. If at any time you read something that makes you feel uncomfortable, this may signify what I am discussing applies to you personally. Pay attention to how you are feeling and be open and honest with yourself. I am no saint, and I'm far from perfect. I am flawed, like every other person on the planet. I also know and believe in my heart that there are many, many good people in this world. Some people say and do things they do not mean and feel bad about it afterward. That is completely okay. We are all a work in progress.

I feel as if I am always trying to accept people for who they are, yet I am constantly being disappointed by human nature. Many people really suck! They complain, they gossip, and they talk about how bad their lives are when, in reality, they are living the American Dream. People are aggressive when driving and are complete bullies behind the wheel. It makes me sick. I have reached a point where I have no choice but to share what I have learned over the past thirty years so I can help people see themselves and the world differently.

I challenge anyone out there to tell me that you are Mother Theresa and love everyone you meet. That's not reality. We need to love one another and stop judging each other. We are all above that, and we can rise above it so we can have a society that is healthy and happy. At the rate we are going, we are doomed as a society unless we stop the hate in the world. We need to love one another and accept one another, warts and all. *We must accept people for who they are and stop judging them for who they are not.* This includes every aspect of every person, including people's respective religions, ethnicity, political views, favorite sports team, and sexual orientation. *We must learn to accept everyone!*

This is serious. Pay attention, and please hear me. Stop kidding yourself and realize that change is within *you*. This is really happening. We have to change. Our lives, the lives of our children, and, most importantly, the lives of our grandchildren and their children depend on it.

This is a no-nonsense guide to help everyone learn to love themselves and one another, and to feel peace and happiness. We are at a crossroads in humanity. We can either continue to hate, or we can choose love. To choose love, we have to be happy from within. We have to love ourselves first to make an impact in this world. In my opinion, this is due to the universal energy that connects all of us. If we are all feeling negative, it is going to spread in ways we cannot even comprehend. Instead, we need to choose to love ourselves first and learn to love one another. Only then can we change the world in which we live.

Okay, rant is over!

Today, my life is wonderful despite the continuous highs, lows, and endless stressors I experience daily. Most likely, I am no different from you. I am a typical American living in the rat race. I get irritated with other people, sometimes I lose my temper, and my patience is constantly being tested. Maybe you will read this and think I am messed up. Or maybe you will read this and realize you can relate to me. My point is that I am constantly trying to get back to a place of peace and happiness, every single day, because life keeps me on my toes! I want to make the most of this life, and it can be hard and stressful.

What helps me get through these daily stressors is the arsenal of tools I use to stay sane in this crazy world. These tools help me get back to a sense of peace and happiness as a result of everything I am about to share with you. I am a very spiritual person, and I felt guided to write this book to help others navigate through their life and maintain their sense of peace and happiness, especially during times of stress and uncertainty, which we all experience in today's world.

For the sake of keeping this book secular, instead of referring to God, I will use the term "Universe" when I wish to refer to a higher power. (The exception is when I am quoting someone else's words.) Call it what you like and what makes sense and feels right to you. I will not refer to any religion throughout this book, as I want to appeal to everyone's humanity regardless of religion, spirituality, or ideology. As I said before, I believe that we are all connected by a universal energy and that every person on this planet deserves to be happy. It is our birthright. It is what the Universe wants for each of us.

The information that I share and the suggested exercises are meant to help you create new habits so you can create lasting change. All the suggested exercises are listed in the order they are introduced at the end of the book. You can choose to write directly in the book, use a separate notebook, or use a computer or tablet for the exercises. If you do every-thing that is suggested, every single day, eventually, it should become second nature to you. That is when lasting change happens. It takes time, patience, and a true desire to create the life you deserve—to feel peace and happiness.

Everything I am discussing needs to be practiced daily. Keep in mind that the word "practice" is key here. There is not one thing in this book that will be mastered. That's not reality. We are human, after all. I will reiterate that the point is to create lasting change so that when life happens, you are armed with the tools to turn your thoughts around and get back to a state of peace and happiness.

The information in this book is listed in a specific order that makes sense to me. It is all useful information that you may feel compelled to read over and over. Jump ahead and read what you need to read when you need it most. By all means, open it up randomly every day and see what pops out at you. Mark the sections that make sense and resonate deeply within you. This is your intuition (a.k.a., your gut) telling you that you are meant to be reading those words. It is all good and is be-ing presented to you in perfect order—exactly when you are meant to see it. That's how life is.

I do want to mention that while I will be sharing some of the most painful moments of my life in this book, part of me feels I have no business writing about my past. There are a bazillion people in this world that have experienced so much worse than I have. There are so many people who struggle in their daily lives, and I could never even imagine what some go through. My experiences seem like a walk in the park com-pared to what they have gone through. I simply share parts of my story to establish that while what I went through was ex-tremely difficult and life-altering, I still have been able to find and maintain a sense of peace and happiness. I'm the person I am today because of my past, as we all are. So no matter what you have been through, no matter what your daily struggles are, you can live a happy and peaceful life as I humbly hope to demonstrate in the pages that follow.

You are about to read this for a reason. There are no coincidences in life. Life is too short for such nonsense.

CHAPTER 2

MY STORY, PART 1: TRAGEDY STRIKES

When I recall my childhood, the happiest memories were when we lived on the Severn River outside of Annapolis, Maryland. I spent my summers on the dock, sunbathing, crabbing, and fishing. My father bought me a small used sailboat when I was old enough to handle it, and I enjoyed many days sailing in the cove with a friend. Although the most fun I had with that little boat involved taking it out without the sails and flipping it over. It was a fun game, rocking it back and forth to see who could balance the longest before falling into the water.

Our house was on a steep hill and there were literally one hundred steps from the dock all the way up to the house. The hill had a few very large trees and ivy overtook the rest. Every time I climbed those steps, I could feel an amazing sense of peace and happiness deep within my heart. I am not sure why I felt this way each time I climbed the hill. Maybe it was the calming effect water had on me, or it could have been how great it felt being in nature. Since I was an athlete, there was also the challenge it presented, along with the sense of accomplishment.

The best day I ever experienced climbing those steps happened was when I was fifteen years old. It was in the middle

8

of winter, and for the first time since we lived there, the river had frozen so deeply it was safe enough to ice skate. I spent an entire day passionately practicing all my jumps, spins, and routines. It was the most amazing experience to escape for hours, doing something I loved more than anything. Climbing the one hundred steps that day made me feel like a rock star!

My journey began after I realized that my life had hit rock bottom. I was depressed and tired of feeling so much pain all the time. Earlier, I mentioned that I'd had my share of life's ups and downs. My biological father died when I was eighteen months old. He worked for the power company in Virginia Beach, Virginia, and was working on live wires when a hot wire touched his ear, and he was killed instantly. He fell on more hot wires, and his body was cremated due to the high voltage. The only thing left of him was his boots and his wallet. As a result, my mother became a widow at age twenty-six, with four children to raise on her own.

While I have no memories of my biological father, I have been told that he loved me very much. My mother used to tell me how, after he passed, I would run up to strangers, asking them if they were my daddy. He had a very dark side to him, so I am told. Every now and then, he would come home drunk and beat my two brothers and my sister with a belt for no reason at all. I have heard many stories about him and his drunken rages. The one story that sticks out is when he pulled out a gun and began shooting the ceiling while threatening my mother. I sometimes speculate how being a witness to such violence affected me. I do think of him often, and I wonder what type of father he would have been to me.

His tragic death brought my family to Baltimore, Maryland. My mother was raised in Baltimore and moved back to be closer to her sister so she would have someone to help her with us kids. At some point after moving, my mother met and married the man who raised me since I was three. Even though he was technically my stepfather, I have always referred to him as my father. He passed away in February of 2016, and I am eternally grateful that he was my father for forty-seven years of my life. I am also extremely grateful for my extended family on his side, which I have had the honor of being a part of ever since I can remember.

My mother used to tell me this story, which has become my favorite. When I was three years old, before my parents married, my father was fixing the wall in the downstairs bathroom. I was trying to help him, and he patiently let me think I was doing my share. My mother heard me asking him if he was going to be my new daddy. She was mortified! My father was a wonderful man who sacrificed so much for all of us. He was a saint to marry my mother with four kids, especially since he had three kids from his previous marriage. My father taught me so much about how to treat other people. He always said that you treat everyone the same—from the janitor to the CEO, treating everyone with kindness. My little brother was born when I was seven, and he was a great kid. To this day, he is still the apple of my eye. When my mother went back to work, I took care of him after school and when my parents went out on the weekends.

Life was pretty good for a long time, until September 30, 1978, when my family experienced another tragic and untimely death. I will never forget that day because I remember feeling so happy for the first time in what seemed like forever. We were living in Severna Park, Maryland, on the Severn River, which I briefly described above. The house was old—we were told that it was originally a post office during the Civil War. It had seen countless transformations over the years, leading up to my family purchasing the home. My father spent many evenings and weekends renovating the house, as it was in bad shape when we moved in.

At some point, my father decided to move the staircase

that led to the basement from one side of the house to the other. While this seemed like a good idea for the long term, in the short term, it caused my older brother and me extreme inconvenience because our bedrooms were in the basement. This meant that we had to go out the side door of the house and around to the front door so we could get to the kitchen and our family room to watch TV. I cannot remember how long it took for the project to be completed, but I do remember it was in the dead of winter.

My parents decided to renew their wedding vows and went away for the weekend for a second honeymoon. Since they were away, I ended up staying with a friend of mine. That particular weekend, we were at her family's cottage home, which was also situated on the Severn River. We were hanging out with her brother and parents when the phone rang. My friend's mom asked me to answer it. I said hello, and a man asked for my friend's mother by her first name. I handed the phone to her, and her face turned serious. She was unsettled about something and would not tell us what was wrong. She just immediately asked her son to take me home by boat, as it would be much faster than a car ride. I was surprised to hear that the man I spoke to was my father. It sounded nothing like him.

The three of us got into their powerboat and rushed to my house, located a few minutes down the river. It was a beautiful warm day, and the ride was exhilarating. I was not that concerned because I figured it probably meant that my grandfather had died. I told my friend this, and we agreed that it probably was that. He had been in and out of the hospital for a long time, and he was aging. The entire family was preparing for his inevitable passing. My friend and I climbed up the one hundred steps from our dock to the side door of my house. We were smiling and laughing, as it was such a steep hill and difficult to climb. My father greeted us at the door, and he politely asked my friend to leave.

I turned and looked at my friend and said goodbye as my heart sank into my stomach. The look on my father's face was one I did not recognize. He started to cry, which is the worst possible thing any daughter can stand to witness: seeing your knight in shining armor break down and cry.

What my father told me was shocking and surreal: my oldest brother, Denny, fell out of a third-story window and died. At first, I thought I was stuck in a horrible nightmare. How was this possible? I was confused and started sobbing uncontrollably, mostly because my father was breaking down. Even though I could not understand what was going on, I could feel the emotions of everyone around me, and I could not control myself. I saw my other older brother, and he just had a blank stare on his face. My mother was inconsolable.

Apparently, he had been on the ground for several hours before anyone noticed. The fall caused the main artery in his heart to burst, so even if he had been found right away, the chances of survival would have been extremely low. He was serving in the US Army and was stationed in Germany. He was only nineteen years old. This changed the course of my entire family's life. I was only twelve years old, and it was two weeks before my thirteenth birthday. Worse yet, because he was in Germany, it took almost three weeks for his body to be returned and for his burial to take place.

The day of the funeral was brutal. The religion in which we were raised holds funeral viewings with an open casket. Per the tradition, you are to walk up to the casket, kneel, and pray for the deceased. My mother asked me to walk up with her, so I obeyed, even though the last thing I wanted to do was see my dead brother lying in a coffin. I remember she said that he looked like a mannequin because there was so much makeup on him. She said he did not look real.

Because the grief and pain was more than I could handle at that age, I made up a story in my mind that he was still alive and that the US Army sent a mannequin to make it look like it was him. Sometimes, the story was that he was in the witness protection program. Other times, he was a spy, and our lives would be in danger if he made contact with us. It was the only thing I could do to push the pain and grief away, and it helped me to make sense of something that made no sense at all.

To this day, once or twice a year, I have a dream about Denny. I open the front door of my house and he's standing there, looking just as I remember him: very tall and hand-some, not really aged at all. In each dream I have, I am in a different house, usually one I do not recognize. We hug, and I say, "I knew you would come back." It is always a pleasant and heartwarming reunion. I never remember the long con-versations we seem to have in my dream, and that is okay. Of course, today, I know that he is gone and is not coming back. However, it is always comforting having him visit me in my dreams. I always wake up with a smile on my face and a sense that we are connected in ways I will never understand.

As a result of this tragedy, I also made up a story about hap-piness. I decided that I could not allow myself to become too happy because if I did, then something horrible would happen. I seriously thought that my happiness would make bad things happen. Back then, it was almost out of the question to seek professional help. So I did the best I could. Instead of dealing with the pain, I lived by the creed "Smile and everything will be okay." While that did work as a temporary fix, what I learned years later was that eventually you do have to deal with the pain.

This journey I have been on has been a quest to find inner peace and happiness and return to the feeling I had while climbing the one hundred steps. It has not always been about just being happy. It has been about being happy when life happens. We all have had the experience of having a fantastic day, and then something happens, and suddenly the happi-ness we were feeling is gone.

CHAPTER 3

WHY ARE WE UNHAPPY?

Before I dive into solving happiness, I think it is best to discuss why we are unhappy and the multitude of triggers that cause unhappiness. Sometimes these triggers cause a state of unhappiness that passes, while other triggers can send you far down the path of unhappiness. While it would be impossible to know all the reasons why people are unhappy, there are certainly enough reasons and triggers we can look at. My goal here is to suggest one or two things that will make sense to you so you have the awareness and tools to turn things around. It breaks my heart to think how many people walk through life unhappy, struggling to hold on. Life is too short to be unhappy.

How does it feel to be unhappy, and what does that mean in terms of our energy levels? When I use the word *energy*, I am not referring to how weak or tired you may be. Nor do I mean the energy you feel from a good night's sleep, a wonderful cup of coffee, or a rigorous exercise session. The energy I am referring to is the electromagnetic field that surrounds us. Most people cannot see this energy field (also referred to as an aura), although some claim they can. However, most people can feel the energy field of those around them if they take the time and pay attention.

Have you ever encountered someone who is in a bad

mood? Chances are you know when people are upset or angry before they say anything. You recognize the way their face looks or their body language, and you likely are feeling something as well. This is because their bad mood has lowered their energy field and they are emitting negative energy waves. The same is true for people with positive energy—they walk into a room, and their energy is so positive that it raises the mood of everyone they meet. Simply put, it does not feel good to be around negative, angry people. However, everyone loves to be around happy people because it feels good.

Stress and Unhappiness

Stress can be a major factor in many people's lives that can easily lead them to feel negative, frustrated, angry, and sad. There are many different types of stress too, which can make life frustrating and certainly not peaceful. At times, you may experience several stressors in one day, while other days, it could be just one.

This can be especially true if you live in a heavily populated area where traffic is a major source of stress. Where I live, traffic is horrible most of the time and is always the first consideration when it comes to determining what time to leave to get to your destination on time. You also hear people saying, "It takes twenty minutes without traffic—an hour with traffic!" Talk about stress! I find that I do not participate in so many things this amazing area has to offer—simply because of the traffic. While the traffic stress I experience does not cause me to be unhappy, it can certainly affect my mood and my peace for short periods.

Another major stressor that more than 80 percent of Americans deal with daily is money, according to a recent survey by Credit Sesame. Also reported in this study is that 40 percent of people feel shame, and roughly 25 percent have cried over their debt situation. Those numbers are staggering! Why is this so?

In my opinion, it is because many people's happiness and self-worth are tied to status symbols such as the house they live in or the car they drive. People worship movie stars, musicians, athletes, and YouTubers and do not feel complete unless they are wearing the latest fashion and have the hottest new technology. While these things can be fun, they provide only temporary fulfillment, leaving you empty in the end with potentially large amounts of debt. I have been guilty of this many times over and can testify that retail therapy is only a temporary solution!

If you are dealing with financial stress, there are plenty of resources out there to help you get back on track. Just be sure that you are not making any poor decisions that are going to take you further down the rabbit hole.

Other stressors can include careers, health issues, relationships, and school. Feeling stressed is not fun and is certainly not the way to live if you desire a happy life. So, if you are not feeling happy, take a look at what areas in your life may be causing you stress. It might not be as obvious as you think.

Stress from traffic is obvious, but you may not realize that your job could be causing you stress, which could, in turn, be causing a strain on your relationships. Whatever stressors are disrupting your peace and happiness, there are tools you can learn to alleviate, eliminate, or lessen the time you are affected.

Here's a more general scenario familiar to many parents. A parent drops the kids off at school, races to the office while eating a high-calorie breakfast, and then works through lunch so she or he can go to the store after work and still be home in time to take their son to basketball practice. Then that parent makes dinner, helps with homework, and puts the kids to bed.

Do you know anyone like this? The parent who thinks you can have it all despite high stress? High stress levels will affect you not only on the inside but also on the outside.

Living with a high amount of stress, no matter the cause, can be damaging to your overall physical health. Stress has been linked to impaired cognitive functioning and serious diseases, not to mention anxiety, depression, and other mental health issues. Stress can also increase your risk for heart disease, as well as cause sleep disorders, hair loss, weight gain, and increased blood pressure. One of the best ways to help reduce stress is to learn how to meditate. I will discuss the benefits of meditation in a later chapter.

Negativity and Unhappiness

Negativity can also be a sign of unhappiness. Have you ever been around someone who is a chronic complainer and is always negative? That person who sees the glass half empty instead of half full? Chances are you know someone like this. This type of person drains the energy out of you like a vampire drinks blood! That negativity pulls you down and literally consumes your energy.

If negative people could learn to change their perspectives on things, they would enjoy life-altering effects. However, they are probably completely unaware of how they show up in this world and the effect they have on themselves and those around them. Being around someone like this all the time can certainly cause you to be unhappy. If this is the case, maybe you should suggest that he or she read this book! If you feel like I am describing you, even if it is just some of the time, keep reading!

Even if you do not feel you are a negative person, have you ever had any negative thoughts? My guess is you likely have on occasion. Negative thinking, even if you do not verbalize the negative thoughts, will still lower your energy. Negative thinking is similar to holding onto anger. It will eat you up inside. Pay attention to when you have a negative thought and switch it to a positive one.

Here is an example. Have you ever thought or said out loud that you hate something or someone? *Hate* is an extremely negative word that will lower your energy. I chose this word because it is so commonly used. If someone says the word *hate*, how many times a day does he or she think it? Do yourself a favor and try to eliminate the word *hate* from your spoken vocabulary *and* your thoughts. The next time you catch yourself thinking about something or someone you hate, correct yourself with a new thought. Instead of thinking, "I hate that movie," you could think, "That movie could have been better." It is a simple shift to be more positive.

Your Actions and Unhappiness

Believe it or not, being unhappy often comes from your own actions. Have you ever taken time to think about the ways you are making yourself unhappy? There are several ways you may be self-inflicting unhappiness, called "triggers."

Creating a Story

The first trigger is a concept I was introduced to by my dear friend Trish called "creating a story". When you create a story, you make assumptions about what you believe is going to happen or what you believe just occurred. It is simply creating a drama in your mind without any facts to base it on.

Here is one example that you may be able to relate to.

Have you ever run into an acquaintance only to have that person blow you off? You may think to yourself, *How rude that she didn't say hello.* This is a story that you made up. You have immediately assumed that this person recognized you and made a conscious effort to avoid you. Maybe that person did choose to avoid you. So what! However, did you ever stop to think that maybe she did not recognize you? Maybe she was having a really bad day and simply did not want to make small talk. You know what? That is completely okay. Stop making it about you! It is not about you! All you are doing is creating a drama that is not there.

Have you ever had someone cut you off in traffic? This is a huge trigger for many people, and some even become violent. Instead of getting mad at the person who almost hit you, how about creating a different story around the situation and not assume that they did it on purpose? Chances are people will not deliberately try to hit someone else's car and risk damaging their own vehicle. You have no idea what circumstances that person is dealing with. There is no way you could possibly know that. Maybe their child was being rushed to the hospital and they were frantically trying to get there. Maybe they were not feeling well and were trying to get somewhere to use the restroom. Or maybe they just did not see you. It happens to everyone at some point or another when you are driving.

You can create a new story to apply to any situation. Whatever it takes to help you feel better at that moment. Create a positive story, or one that is not about you, so you can get rid of the negative thinking that is causing you so much misery.

I had a "story" that I told myself over and over, for years on end. The story was that my husband (now ex-husband) was going to die. He traveled a lot, so every time he got on an airplane, I imagined it was going to crash. Whenever he was late, I imagined he was in a car accident. It was a

19

horrible existence that I created in my mind. After many years of therapy, I learned that I had a form of post-traumatic stress disorder (PTSD) stemming from the tragic loss of my brother.

It was a struggle, but I eventually learned to calm myself down because it was something completely out of my control. I realized that I was creating this drama without any reason and it was causing me to feel anxious and miserable for close to two decades. While I sometimes fall back into this pattern, it happens less frequently now that I am armed with many tools to turn it around.

The point is, once you are aware that you are creating a story, you have the power to stop thinking that way. Pay attention to your thoughts, and when you realize you are creating a story that simply is not true, gently tell yourself that you are making this up because there are no facts on which to base it.

Think about a situation where you have created a story. Pay attention to how it makes you feel and if any negative emotions are festering. When you think of the situation, is it one based on true facts? Consider that maybe you have made an assumption, especially if it involves how another person is feeling or thinking. What other story can you attach to the situation instead? Change the story surrounding it and see if you feel better.

Criticizing Yourself

How many times a day (or week) do you criticize yourself? This is a common theme that many people learn from our childhood peers and family members. For those of you who have children, have you ever criticized yourself in front of your children? If you have, you are teaching them to do the same. It is that negative self-talk, which, in my opinion, is a learned behavior.

During a recent visit to spend time with my brother and his family, I heard my niece say to herself, "I am such an idiot."

I immediately turned to her with a serious look and said, "Please stop calling my niece an idiot!"

She had a stunned expression on her face. Then, realizing what I had just said, she started laughing. I tend to use that often with my friends and family as a way to point out that they are criticizing themselves and I do not like it. It is offensive to hear my loved ones be so critical of themselves. If you keep criticizing yourself over and over, eventually, you are going to believe it.

Growing up, I remember being teased all the time. It was as if I had this sign on my forehead, asking for it. I was teased a lot because of my turned-up nose. I was even bullied over it. As a result of this bullying and teasing, I was self-conscious about my nose for most of my life and thought it made me look ugly. In my early forties, I made an appointment with a plastic surgeon to transform my nose into what I imagined looked to be the perfect straight nose.

The doctor took a picture of my face and my profile and showed me on the computer what I might look like after the surgery. I was mortified! It was then that I fully accepted my beautiful nose. It made me unique and different. This was a turning point for me. Later, I am going to discuss acceptance, which will be instructive for those who habitually talk negatively to themselves.

I was teased so much as a child that I ended up not liking myself for many years. It makes perfect sense when you think about it. If people you like constantly make fun of you, what is a child to think? I was on a constant quest to gain everyone's approval and was extremely critical of myself. I eventually learned about self-love, and I realized that not loving myself was a huge part of why I was unhappy for so long—so much so that I could not wait to get married so I could drop my maiden name. For years, I did not like that person. By taking my husband's name, I became a new person, had a new identity.

It took me many years to finally embrace who I am. I am finally proud to be her and to love and accept all that she was, is, and will be. I am the person I am today because of everything I have endured, and I would not change a thing. I have learned to embrace my past and not be saddened or ashamed by it.

What Other People Think of You

One trigger that so many people inflict upon themselves is that they constantly worry what other people think of them. If you think about it, young toddlers could not care less if they were walking around with a smelly diaper! However, if that same child was in kindergarten and had an accident, other children would probably laugh and tease them about it. What effect is that going to have on the child? They are going to be subconscious about being smelly. They end up being more concerned about what other people think.

What about the child that is overweight? They also could not care less, until they hear someone, possibly a stranger, another child, or a loved one make a comment about their size. It is then that the child begins to look at themselves negatively. In this case, education is necessary to teach the child healthy eating and exercise habits. As adults, we are responsible for nurturing children and teaching them about self-love and not to be concerned with what other people think of them. My good friend Sonja used to remind me, "What other people think of you is none of your business!" I share this statement as a reminder and an affirmation to keep handy.

When you think about it, if you are concerned about what other people think about you, how does that affect your ability to love yourself? The next time you become aware that you are worried about what other people think about you, please stop yourself right there. Be gentle with yourself. Repeat to yourself at least ten times, "I love, respect, and honor my true self, exactly the way I am. I am perfectly human."

After having said all that, there are some situations where it may be important to mind what other people think of you. For instance, when you are interviewing for a new job, it is important that you make a good impression. If you are interested in having a romantic partner, you are obviously going to be concerned about what they think of you. I could give many more examples, and I trust that you get the point. Just remember to use your best judgment in every situation. At the end of the day, the important thing is not to let your peace and happiness be disrupted. This is where trust comes into play, which will be discussed in a later chapter.

Criticizing or Judging Others

Have you ever criticized or judged another person? Most likely, you have. Everyone does it at one point or another. While there are some psychological theories that explain why people criticize and judge others (I will not discuss these, as I am not an expert in that area), it is simply a bad idea if you want to be happy.

Criticizing and judging others is negative and will lower your energy. How do you think the other person would feel if they knew you were so critical or judgmental of them? Most likely, you would be hurting their feelings. Turn the tables around and imagine how you would feel if someone said the same about you. You probably would be hurt as well. If you are thinking these thoughts—or, even worse, saying them out loud—catch yourself and replace them with a positive thought about the situation. It will take time to get into the habit of changing your thoughts and eventually, it will become second nature.

Worrying

Another way that people cause their own unhappiness is by chronically worrying about things that are either within or outside their control. I heard a speaker once say, "If you can control it, then stop worrying about it because you can control it. If you cannot control it, then stop worrying about it because you cannot control it." You are wasting your precious time if you are worried about anything. I am not suggesting that you throw your hands in the air and proclaim, "F**k everything." You obviously have to think things through and take action when necessary. The important thing to note here is that the only thing you can control is your own thoughts and actions and how you react to people and situations.

Some worry excessively that they are going to become sick with a disease or other health condition. Can you control this? Yes and no. You can control how you take care of yourself by eating healthy, exercising, and having regular checkups with your primary care physician. Otherwise, you have no choice but to trust that everything will work out exactly the way it was meant to be. I will also discuss trust later in great detail.

Comparing Yourself to Others

Have you ever thought that comparing yourself to someone else is a dangerous place to go? If you are comparing yourself to someone else and thinking, *If I had their looks/social status/ wealth, then I would be happy*, then you are simply making up a story. My close friend Michele explained it beautifully once. She said that if you compare yourself to another person and tell yourself you wish you were them, you had better be willing to accept 100 percent of all the good *and* all the bad in that person's life. Think about that for a minute. Everyone has their own share of faults, traumas, insecurities, and ups and downs. It is much easier to accept yourself and stop putting so much energy toward that type of thinking.

Jealousy

Jealousy is another poison that will rot you to the core. It makes my skin crawl when I hear someone say they are jealous of someone else. Please remove this word from your vocabulary and be happy for the other person.

Pay attention to when jealous thoughts come up or jealous statements come out of your mouth. Remember what I said about comparing yourself to others. While you may be jealous of someone else's accomplishments—the car they drive, the money they have, or the beautiful shoes they are wearing—just know that the person you are feeling jealous of has their own issues, pain, and struggles that you are not even aware of. They are not perfect, and neither are you.

Social Media

Social media is another outside trigger than can cause much unhappiness. I honestly cannot imagine growing up in today's world. Things are so much more complicated. While I enjoy being on Facebook and Instagram, mainly to see what my close friends and family are up to, it is not the healthiest place to spend your precious time. In fact, some social media platforms are changing so that only the author of a post can see how many likes their post has received. I do not post very much, and I look at Facebook only a few times a week. I find I am much happier not reading political posts and some of the angry things I see people post.

Let's face it, social media can be addictive. In fact, there are studies that show how social media has increased the depression and suicide rates, especially in teens and young adults. Social media platforms use predictive analytics to target its users. It is actually quite scary. One way to avoid the constant need to view the content on these platforms is to turn off the notification settings on your device so you are not constantly drawn to them.

If you are a person who likes to post on social media and engage in conversation, please pay attention to what you are posting. Once it is out there, it stays out there. Also, please avoid posting anything negative. I am constantly surprised at how mean people are in their online conversations. If you feel compelled to lash out at someone, seriously think about it before doing so. Ask yourself if you would say the same thing to the person if you were face to face with them. Next, ask yourself how you would feel if someone made a similar comment to you online. I am guessing most of the bullies on the internet would not say the same thing to someone's face and that they would feel horrible if someone made a nasty comment to them. Be kind to everyone, especially online!

Be Yourself

Be yourself! When you are not yourself, you are likely not happy. I could see this in many of my son's friends, which is common for teenagers (and many adults), who are still trying to figure out who they are. They may participate in things just to fit in with others, while deep down, they know it is not who they really are.

The next time you are about to do something that may be outside your comfort zone, do a "gut" check with yourself. How does it feel? Is it something that you will truly enjoy, or are you doing it to be seen by others or feel like you fit in? Do yourself a favor and be true to who you are. Being true to yourself will make you feel so good. Besides, who cares what other people think of you? You do not need anyone else's approval. Once again, what other people think about you is none of your business.

I Cannot Change

Have you ever heard someone say that this is the way they are and they cannot change? I have seen this many times with people. That is being stubborn! Everyone can change. Heraclitus, the Greek philosopher, said, "Change is the only constant in life." Everything is constantly changing around us.

So if you think you are incapable of change, you are doing yourself a huge disservice. You are an incredible, intelligent human being who is 100 percent capable of change. However, only you are responsible for making a change in your life. Others cannot do it for you. Many people simply get into a rhythm and keep doing the same thing over and over. They may not even recognize that their habits are causing them pain and misery.

How often do you do the same thing, over and over, thinking you will have a different outcome? Can you recognize a pattern in your behavior? I am going to use the example of yo-yo dieting, as this is an issue for so many people (myself included): You start a diet plan, and you do not get the results you are expecting. You may lose a little weight, but not enough, so you go back to your previous eating habits and gain more weight. Repeat. You are not getting the instant gratification that you are expecting. That is insanity at its finest!

Self-Sabotage

Most people know that drugs, alcohol, and gambling are triggers and that their abuse can cause a state of unhappiness. However, when someone is in the midst of one of these addictions, it may not be so obvious. There are plenty of other bad habits that can cause you to be unhappy. Overeating is a bad habit that affects millions of people worldwide. At the same time, many people suffer from eating disorders. If you believe that you are abusing drugs or alcohol, you have a gambling problem, or you have an eating disorder, please seek the advice of a medical professional or join a support group. Getting help and recovering from the addiction or disorder is your first step. This book will be here to help you when you are ready.

I sincerely hope that at least one item discussed in this chapter stands out. I have experienced most of them at some point in my life. While each of these things on their own may not cause too much unhappiness, over time, unhappiness can build up.

Do you want to live your life to the fullest? You are worth it, and so is your life! It is too short for anything less than being happy.

CHAPTER 4

MY STORY, PART 2: MY DARKEST MOMENTS

When I talked about my life hitting rock bottom previously, that was an understatement, to say the least. Soon after I moved to Washington, D.C., when I was twenty years old, I let the dark side into my life. I had been introduced to drugs multiple times since my early teen years, and I had only tried marijuana. I did not like the feeling it gave me, so I rarely used it. I am not sure when the moment of weakness arrived, as my life had been going great. I remember it was a work night, and I was hanging out with some friends. One of them pulled out some cocaine, and I immediately said, "No way." Eventually, I gave in and tried it. That was the worst decision I have made in my entire life.

For a while, I used it only when my friends had it, as it was not something that I could afford. However, cocaine's ability to grip and control whoever decides to use it multiple times will turn anyone's life upside down. I was no different. In March of 1987, I met my future husband and hid my cocaine use from him.

A few years went by, and I continued using it when I could, while still hiding it from my boyfriend. At this point, we were living together. I remember multiple times, I would be lying in bed, and my heart would be racing so fast that I was convinced I was going to have a heart attack.

I remember the pain I felt talking to my mother after my brother passed. She was so worried that he was not in heaven and wondered if he asked for forgiveness of his sins before his accident. The religion in which I was raised dictated that you must ask for forgiveness of your sins every night before going to sleep to ensure you would be welcomed into heaven. There were many nights when I was high on cocaine, my heart racing a mile a minute, and I hoped I would not wake up. I would ask for forgiveness of my sins because I was so sure I would not wake up. I just wanted the pain to go away. I would wake the next morning with a sense of disappointment that I had to struggle through another day.

At the end of 1989, my boyfriend and I became engaged, and I was hopeful that my life would begin to turn around. The problem with that scenario is that I continued to use cocaine, and my fiancé still had no idea. In January of 1990, my fiancé was on a business trip, and he was unable to reach me. He ended up coming home early, as he was so worried about me.

I arrived home after being gone for over twenty-four hours and was greeted by him. He thought that I had been with another man. I would never have cheated on him and had to admit that I had been using cocaine. He was furious with me. An hour later, my mother and father arrived. They talked it through with both of us, and I agreed to get the help I needed.

I went through a six-month voluntary outpatient recovery program. The very first session, I was told that I also had to give up drinking alcohol. Alcohol was not my drug of choice, and it never seemed to be an issue for me, so I gladly gave up everything so I could focus on recovery and healing. Another requirement of the outpatient therapy was to attend a support group. I tried Cocaine Anonymous and Narcotics Anonymous and did not like either one. My counselor suggested I try

Alcoholics Anonymous and referred me to a women's group. I went to a meeting and instantly felt like I was home. I was told that even if I did not feel as though I was an alcoholic, the twelve steps and AA community were always open to anyone who needed to recover from anything.

My fiancé and I got married in June of 1991, and life was really good. I was completely sober, and there were times when cocaine would show its power over me, even after not using it for over a year and a half. I remember driving home from work one day and out of the blue, I could smell its very distinct scent. That was when I completely understood the importance of not using any type of substance whatsoever. I was afraid to take a sip of alcohol for fear that I would be tempted to use cocaine. I never wanted to see that horrible drug again and the viscous cycle that my life became while using it.

The years that followed, I found my deep connection with the Universe, worked the twelve steps, and my life began to change. I learned how to get back to the feeling I had when I was climbing the one hundred steps. There was an endless light in my tunnel, and all I had to do was look up and keep climbing. I had a sense of peace, happiness, and serenity. My life finally had a purpose, and all I wanted to do was help other people.

CHAPTER 5

LIFE HAPPENS

What does everyone want? To be happy! Many believe that as soon as they get one or all of these things, they will be happy:

more money
a new car
a new partner
a new house
a better job
a _____ (fill in the blank)

How would you feel if you had those things? I imagine that you think those things would make you happy. Having all those things can certainly make life easier or perhaps more comfortable. However, I promise you, those things do not and cannot make you happy. Maybe you will be happy for a short period, and at some point, you will be searching for something else to make you happy. The keyword there is "something else."

Ever heard of the term "retail therapy"? Many men and women go shopping as a means of seeking happiness. For a short time, you feel good. You bought a new pair of shoes or a new outfit, and it feels so good. It is merely a temporary fix. It works in the moment, until you realize you have maxed out your credit cards or spent money on things you really did not need. Then you do not feel so good. I have been there—many, many times.

Years ago, my ex-husband bought me a new car because he was hoping that would make me happy. We were going through a rough patch, and he knew I was not happy with our relationship. I had always dreamed of having a convertible. After much resistance on my part, I agreed to go buy the car. I went to the dealership, and they had a brand new white convertible with a navy blue top. It was the most beautiful car I had ever seen! We did all the paperwork, and the next day, he dropped me off to pick up the car. That particular day, I had planned a trip to go see my parents. So I got into my new dream car and drove three hours to the beach to see my mom and dad. I put the top down and just drove. It was amazing! I finally had the car I had always wanted. I felt so happy. Do you want to know how long that feeling lasted? About three hours! I arrived at my parents, showed the car off, and said to my mom, "I am still not happy."

Now, some of you might be thinking that I sound like a spoiled brat. What I am saying here is that while it was wonderful to be driving my dream car, a car cannot make me or anyone else happy. Things cannot make you happy—not a new car, not a new house, not a new job, and especially not money. All they bring is temporary satisfaction.

I grew up in a large family. While our needs were always met, I remember seeing my parents struggle. I married well and lived a very comfortable life for over twenty years. Then I went through a divorce, and I struggled to make ends meet. Now that I am remarried, I live on a strict budget. My point is that I have been poor, rich, and back to a place where I make enough to live and I am happy! Money cannot bring happiness. I have lived that lesson several times over. I have learned how to be happy. It is not because of things. It is not because

I have an amazing son and husband. It is because I learned, over the course of twenty-five years of being in a relationship that was not right for me—constantly soul searching and reading, attending workshops, therapy sessions, life coaching sessions, and so on—that happiness comes from within. I learned that I am the only person who can make *me* happy.

Throughout this book, I am going to present you specific steps you can take to find your happiness, your joy, your peace. I am going to show you how to stay happy when life throws you curveballs.

> Peace. It is not about being in a place where there is no trouble, noise or hard work. It means to be in the midst of those things and still be calm in your heart.
>
> —Author Unknown

This is my favorite quote. Does that resonate with you? Do you fully understand it? Many people think that finding peace means simply eliminating trouble, noise, and hard work from your life. Quite the contrary. It is easy to feel peaceful and happy when you are having a quiet weekend or taking a walk in nature. So, how can you maintain that feeling when you are sitting in traffic? How can you maintain a sense of peace when you are living the rat race? That is what everyone is searching for. This is why you max out your credit cards or escape with your phone for hours on end or maybe turn to less-than-healthy things as a means of escape—drugs, alcohol, or gambling. Humans are constantly searching for happiness, and we keep looking in all the wrong places.

Years ago, when I was a stay-at-home mom, I found I needed more stimulation, so I started my life coaching career. I felt inspired to write and ended up writing two novels, one of which was a finalist for two book awards. I presented workshops, coached clients, and produced and hosted a BlogTalkRadio show that aired for two years. My life has always been about helping other people. It gives me satisfaction and is my life's purpose.

I remember how peaceful my life was. However, I was not really living in the rat race. I was a witness to it. I once heard a speaker say, "It is easy to stay in a peaceful place when we are just going to the grocery store and not really dealing with many people. The difference is when we are in the midst of all the craziness in the world. That is when our peace and happiness are tested." Wow, was she right!

When I got divorced, I needed to have a consistent income, so I went back to work full-time. That is when my peace and happiness were really tested. It took me a couple of years to get back to my previous state of inner peace. It was frustrating learning to navigate through all of life's ups and downs, which I hadn't experienced in many years.

I have been a student of life for over thirty years, almost to an extreme. I have read hundreds of books, listened to hundreds of audio lectures, and attended countless seminars. I have spent thousands of dollars on therapy sessions and life-coaching sessions. I have learned how to be happy.

I am not going to tell you that living a happy life is easy or that you just need to think positive. You are an intelligent person, which is why you have made an investment in the most important person in your life—*you*! Some people think it is narcissistic to believe that you are the most important person in your life. It is actually the opposite. Do you want to be a good mother/father, husband/wife, son/daughter, sister/brother, friend, employee, or lover? My guess is that you do. You have purchased this book because you want to be happy and improve yourself. You want more out of life. So, let me ask you this: How do you think you can be a good mother/father, husband/wife, son/daughter, sister/brother, friend, employee, or lover if you are not taking care of *you*? If you want to be all of those things, then you *must* take care of yourself first.

In the past thirty years of my life, I have been on mission—to find a way to live *my* life and *be* happy. I have had more than my share of life's ups and downs, so I bring to you all the tools I have acquired to help you navigate through life with a happy heart, regardless of your circumstances or how bad you *think* things are.

My mission began as the result of many things. For the most part, I have always been happy. However, an event took place that was the catalyst to change how I viewed myself and the world around me. Most people make major shifts in life only following a major life event. My friend, I do not want you to wait for such an event to experience all that joy that life is. Life is too short for that. It is here and gone in what seems like an instant.

Understand that you are the only person responsible for your happiness. There is no one to blame for your lack of happiness except you. A teacher of mine once said, "When you are pointing your finger at someone else, remember that there are three fingers pointing right back at you." I am guessing you just stopped reading to test that for yourself! It is a very simple yet powerful thing to remember. You see, the only thing that can affect your personal happiness is how you perceive the world around you and, more importantly, how you choose to react to your perception of the situation. The key phrase is "how you choose to react to your perception." It is easy to blame someone else for your lack of happiness. Have you ever thought, *If only I had a better job, I would be happy?* or *If only I had more money, I would be happy?* Really? If you think your job or your money is responsible for your happiness, then we have a lot of work to do, my friend! Neither a new job nor all the money in the world can bring you happiness. You, and only you, can create the inner peace, the happiness that everyone wants so badly. As I said before, I am not going to tell you that living a happy life is easy. What is easy is what I am about to share with you. The tools I discuss in this book are easy. The hard part is remembering to practice them when "life happens" so you are able to retain that inner peace and happiness.

No one is perfect, and while I am generally happy, I have my moments too—I am human. However, I have learned to use these tools in my daily life, and I have done so for so many years that when life happens, my peace is not interrupted for very long. As a friend of mine used to say, "Life happens while we're busy making other plans." So, how can you maintain your sense of peace and happiness when experiencing life's curveballs?

CHAPTER 6

TAKING CARE OF YOU!

Take care of *you*. I believe this is the most important step of living a happy life, which is why I am discussing it first. However, it can be the hardest step to achieve. When you are taking care of everyone else around you that is when you must take time for yourself. As I mentioned earlier, if you want to be good mother/father, husband/wife, son/daughter, sister/brother, friend, employee, or lover, then taking care of yourself is critical. Why? Because if you do not take care of yourself, you are not going to be a good mother/father, husband/wife, son/daughter, sister/brother, friend, employee, or lover.

What exactly does this mean? It means you have to take the time to take care of your personal needs, do something special for yourself, and possibly say "no" to someone else. This doesn't mean that you are not going to feed your children or take care of things you need to do at your job. Everyone has something, someone, or multiple people they are responsible for taking care of.

This means you have to take the time to do things for yourself that make *you* feel good. And I am not talking about the obvious things, like taking a shower or brushing your teeth. It is going to mean something different for everyone. Maybe it means that you need to make time to see your friends each week. Maybe it is simply taking a hot bath before you go to bed. Whatever it means to you, you must find time every day to do something special for yourself. There may be days when you can only fit in ten to twenty minutes. That's okay.

Awhile back, I remembered that I really missed starting my day with some quiet time with just me and my coffee. I began setting my alarm for twenty minutes earlier to allow for this quiet time before I started my day. It was a little hard at first, and after a week of getting up twenty minutes earlier, it was easy. Now I am used to it, and every day, I sit in the kitchen by myself and enjoy that first cup of coffee.

For me, it sets the tone for the day as I feel centered and I do not start my day rushing around. Some days I will read some inspirational material, and other days, I simply sit and enjoy the silence of the morning. What I learned is that by starting my day this way, I feel really good knowing that I already did one thing for me, and it feels so good!

A few years ago, I realized I was not spending any time with my friends. My life became so busy with a move into a new house, and my son's activities increased, so I unintentionally stopped taking the time to see my friends. Spending time with your close friends is something that should not be taken for granted. As humans, we need a connection with other people. I am blessed to be married to an amazing man, and I also have my son.

However, I became caught up with taking care of them and everything else going on in my life, and I simply did not make the time. Once again, it became a void in my life. But, you see, this is part of the process of figuring out how to take care of yourself. It will change from time to time. During my busy schedule, I did not even notice that I had put my friends on the back burner. When my life started to settle down, that is when it became apparent that I really missed my "girlfriend time." I read a study once that said women live longer when they have girlfriends! As a matter of fact, today, I see my girlfriends at least twice a week, sometimes more. I am having the time of my life, and I absolutely treasure my girlfriend time. I schedule it in advance and have made it a priority.

There are several things that are very simple and can be done every day that will improve your chances of staying grounded and feeling good. Have you ever heard of a "news fast"? It is a concept I learned about years ago. I used to watch the local news every morning while having a cup of coffee or getting ready for my day. I started to notice how, after watching the news, I did not feel very good. I would find myself thinking about all the problems that were going on in my state, in the country, and throughout the world.

I decided to try a "news fast," and it was amazing how different I began to feel not knowing how many people had been murdered the day before or hearing about disasters that took place on the other side of the world. I am not saying you do not need to be informed. However, is there anything that you can do to change what took place? Nope. So why let it bring you down?

Instead of watching the morning news, try reading affirmations. Affirmations are short statements that, if you read them a few times, can raise your energy and help you get into a state of feeling good. There are hundreds of books that contain all sorts of affirmations directed at men, women, spiritual people, religious people, and so on. Find one that speaks to you, and refer to it whenever you need it most. If you have a smartphone, go online and do a search for affirmations. You will find that the one you need to see will appear when you need it the most.

One of the things I tend to do is keep my environment clutter free. Clutter can be stacks piled-up mail, clothes that need to be put away, or anything else that is disorganized. Cleaning up the clutter is another way to take care of yourself. For me, clutter and disorganization cause anxiety, taking up space in my head.

While this may not apply to you, pay attention to how you feel the next time you are in an area that is cluttered and messy. Taking the time to organize your life, whether it is your garage, your closet, or your kitchen, is a way to take control when many things seem uncontrollable. If you reach a point where you feel like everything is out of your control, which can easily happen in this chaotic world, try decluttering a room or closet. It is such a good feeling knowing that you did something else for yourself.

Years ago, I took a meditation course that changed my life. When you meditate, you will reduce stress, relax your body, and calm your mind. Recent medical studies have shown that regular meditation can have the following benefits:

- Heart disease patients reduced their risk of having another heart attack by 74 percent.
- Approximately 77 percent of individuals with high stress levels were able to lower their blood pressure.
- Roughly 75 percent of long-term insomniacs were able to fall asleep within twenty minutes after meditation.
- After four months of consistent meditation, your body will produce less of the hormone cortisol, thus adapting to stress no matter what the situation. This results in better eating habits.

So, the next time you feel compelled to work a full eight hours and then proceed to overschedule your one-hour break before throwing a dinner party, think about feeding your soul instead and meditate! By incorporating a meditation practice into your daily routine, you can improve the health of your mind and body.

Spending time in nature is one of the best medicines for taking care of yourself and bringing a sense of peace and tranquility to your mind. A recent article in *Time* magazine, written by Jamie Ducharme, stated, "Spending time outdoors, especially in green spaces, is one of the fastest ways to improve your health and happiness. It is been shown to lower stress, blood pressure and heart rate."

Everyone needs something that they are passionate about—something that gives their life more purpose. I am not going to just tell you to find your passion or purpose, because I feel like having a passion and purpose is something that you may stumble upon. I am passionate about writing, although I had no idea until I was an adult. Now, writing has become my purpose in life, among other things. I was never one to write in a journal; nor did I ever attempt to write anything until I was in my forties. It was something I stumbled upon. However, if you can find something you are passionate about and gives your life greater purpose, it will become something else you can do that makes you feel really good.

I suggest making a list of things that are of interest to you and, each week, learn more about it, research it, or sign up for a class. Many schools and community centers have a variety of classes, and there just may be something that sparks your interest. Many times, you can learn how to do something by looking on YouTube. For me, I have a bucket list of things that I want to try at some point in my life. This includes learning how to paint, arrange flowers, play the guitar, salsa and/or ballroom dancing, among other things. Whatever it is for you, please do not delay trying to find something that excites you. It will be one more way to take good care of yourself.

While this book is meant to help you find your peace and happiness and not about health and fitness, taking care of your body, on the inside and out, is another way to take care of yourself. I am sure you have heard the saying "You are what you eat." Those words are very, very true. Food can have an effect on your mood. Look at processed sugar, for example. Processed sugar is lethal to our body, causing your insulin levels to spike and then fall. I am by no means an expert on nutrition; however, I do know enough to watch everything I am consuming. I love to eat, so I generally do not eliminate things from my diet. I try to avoid the food choices that are obviously bad for my health. I simply eat the things I love in moderation, so I do not deny myself one of life's simple pleasures!

Getting enough sleep every single night is also a critical part of taking care of yourself and one that is a priority for me. When we sleep, our bodies can rejuvenate. There are numerous studies that discuss the many benefits of getting a restful night's sleep, as well as the damage that can be caused from sleep deprivation. For me personally, having a good night's sleep sets the tone for every single day of my life.

As for exercise, it is yet another activity that will make you feel really good. I do not have much time to exercise, so I try to squeeze it in when I can. I have been extremely active my entire life, and I encourage you to find that one activity where you can get your heart rate up and enjoy yourself at the same time.

So, what do you need to do to put yourself first? The best way to figure this out is to write down all the things that would make you happy and feel super good. These are things that you may not do regularly. Maybe it is taking a hot bath with a lot of candles lit, taking a walk in nature, or learning something you have always wanted to learn. Take care of yourself first—life is too short for anything less!

CHAPTER 7

THE "F" WORD

The "F" word I am about to reveal can be a touchy subject to some. I believe—and know with every beat of my heart—that the "F" word is at the core of finding happiness. I know this is true because it was something I had to learn how to do. It is something that I still have to practice. In some circumstances, I have to remind myself every day, sometimes every hour, every minute, to practice. On the surface, it seems it would not be that hard to perfect. However, I am always amazed at how hard it can be. Sometimes, things from the past resurface, and I realize that I still need to practice the "F" word. It can be a cycle that needs to be repeated over and over.

I am dragging this out for dramatic effect, as I want to really make a point with this topic. I am sure most people know by now what I am referring to, so I will spell it out:

Forgiveness

Side note: I am referring to forgiveness from a human perspective, not from a religious perspective. I believe that forgiveness is something that is imperative for everyone, and it has nothing to do with religion (even though it is mentioned throughout religious writings).

I mentioned earlier that happiness is connected to peace. When we are at peace, we feel happy. It feels really good. Our energy is in a higher state. When we are not feeling complete peace in our heart, there is someone or something that needs to be forgiven. So what does forgiveness have to do with being happy? As I said, I believe that forgiveness is at the core of finding one's happiness. Practicing forgiveness is yet another way to drastically shift your energy from negative to positive.

There are two parts of forgiveness that need to be practiced. I am going to discuss forgiving other people first. Every single person on the planet has been in the midst of some situation in which they have had their feelings hurt or is upset with another person because of something they did or said.

I recently had a conversation with a young man who clearly resented his father. I started talking to him about forgiveness and that it would be the only way he would feel better and be able to have a truly loving and healthy relationship with his dad. He just kept shaking his head and saying, "No way." I let it go, because not everyone is ready to accept forgiveness and the power it has on their life. I respected this fact and did not push the topic any further.

You see, many people believe that if you forgive another person for their actions, you are therefore letting them off the hook, saying it is okay that they did what they did. This is so far from the truth. If you are holding resentment toward another person, how does this affect you and your peace and happiness? Resentment is another form of anger. It is like a disease that will eat you up inside and make you miserable. Why would anyone want to live like that? If you are holding on to anger and bitterness, not only will it affect you physically, but it will also hold you back from experiencing any sort of happiness.

Check in with yourself and think of a person who did something to you. How does it feel? If you are feeling anything but love for this person, then you are likely still holding on to resentment.

Forgiving another person is not about letting them off the hook and saying what they did or said to you is okay. When you resent someone, all you are doing is letting them take up space in your head. Why would you want to take your own power away and give it to them? Do you really want to keep them in your thoughts, reliving what they did over and over? I sure hope not. What a miserable way to live. Life is too short to be miserable.

Forgiving another person is all about freeing yourself of the misery that you let them cause you. Yes, you read that correctly. You are letting them cause you misery. Why? Because you control your thoughts, not them. You have the power to release the resentment and take your power back. If someone did something to hurt you, why would you want to give them that power? You are giving them what they want if you are letting them use up all of that real estate in your head. Understand that while you are not responsible for what they did to you, you are responsible for how you react, meaning, if you are holding onto the miserable feelings that their actions caused, those feelings you are holding onto are your responsibility. Holding onto those feelings is causing you misery. It is your responsibility, and you owe it to yourself, to forgive and let it go.

I realize that many people have been through horrible things, in which another person has inflicted pain on them. I am not in any way trying to minimize anyone's pain; nor am I suggesting forgiving someone who hurt you is always easy. In some situations, it might be something you think about every day, every hour, or every minute until you are able to truly forgive. In some cases, it could take a very long time. That is perfectly okay. As I said, you may have to focus on forgiving someone or something over and over. Eventually, you will be free.

One powerful story of forgiveness is hard to forget, especially as a parent. In October 2006, Charles Roberts walked into an Amish schoolhouse in Pennsylvania armed with three guns. He shot ten girls, killing five of them, before killing himself. Even though Charles had committed this horrific crime, the Amish community and the loved ones of the deceased demonstrated forgiveness in a way that most could never imagine. They attended Charles's funeral and comforted his widow. Charles's mother, Terri Roberts, stated, "For the mother and father who had just lost not one but two daughters at the hand of our son, to come up and be the first ones to greet us—wow. Is there anything in this life that we should not forgive?"

The second part of forgiveness is forgiving yourself. This is so important because humans are generally very hard on themselves. Every single person on the planet has likely done something to make them feel bad about themselves. The key here is to be mature enough to admit it to yourself and be okay with it. We are perfectly human.

When you are holding on to negative feelings toward yourself, they will affect your ability to love yourself. Self-love is critical to feeling peace and happiness. Here are some examples of things you may have done in which forgiveness is necessary:

- Have you ever been hard on yourself?
- Have you ever done something to hurt someone else's feelings?
- Have you broken a promise to yourself?
- Have you broken a promise to someone else?
- Have you ever been resentful of someone or something?
- Have you ever been jealous of someone else?

In each of the examples above, think about how you feel when you remember a situation. Forgiving yourself is no different from forgiving another. However, it can be much harder. For me, this is because I can be so hard on myself, and it becomes such a normal part of my existence. The key to self-forgiveness is recognizing in the moment when you are thinking negative thoughts about yourself or someone else.

Whenever you forgive someone else, you may need to forgive yourself as well. Here's an example of what I am thinking when I am sitting next to someone who is chewing their food loudly: *I wish he wouldn't chew his food so loudly. Oh my God, it is so noisy! Okay, I am sorry. I forgive him for being a loud eater, and I forgive myself for being so critical of him.* As I mentioned earlier, you may have to repeat your statement over and over until the feelings of irritability, anger, or resentment dissipate.

Even if the self-sabotage occurs only in your thoughts, you still need to forgive yourself. This is because your negative thoughts are going to spread. It is kind of like a virus. The more you think negative thoughts, the more negative thoughts you will think. You can stop the negative pattern simply by being aware of your thoughts. I highly recommend you do all the exercises listed at the end of the book and record your thoughts and actions that apply to each area listed. It will make forgiveness that much easier for you. Life is too short to hold on to negativity, resentment, and anger. Forgive instead!

CHAPTER 8

THE POWER OF GRATITUDE

It's not having what you want, it's wanting what you've got.

—Sheryl Crow

That is one of my favorite lines in Sheryl Crow's song, "Soak Up the Sun." It is completely true! That's how gratitude is. There is an amazing feeling that will consume every inch of your being when you take the time to just be grateful. I remember my father making me finish eating everything on my plate because there were "starving kids all over the world." While that may not be the best idea for teaching healthy eating habits, it taught me that there is always someone who has it worse off than I do. Nowadays, you hear people saying "First World problems." There is so much truth to that. People are always complaining about what they do not have or complaining about their horrible circumstances. Do any of these statements sound familiar:

- "I had to wait for three hours for the plumber to show up to fix my toilet."
- "Can you believe it took the waiter ten minutes to serve our drinks?"
- "It took forty-five minutes for my food to be delivered, and it was not hot."

Those are First World problems! Instead of complaining about waiting for three hours for the plumber to show up, be grateful that you have the resources to fix your indoor plumbing problems. Instead of complaining that the waiter took too long to serve your drinks, be grateful that you are being served and give the waiter an extra tip. Instead of complaining about how long it took for your food to be delivered, be grateful that you got to stay in the comfort of your own home while someone else cooked and delivered your food, and give the delivery person an extra tip. I hope you get the point! These are real-life things that have happened millions of times. In the moment, it certainly can be frustrating, and remember, there are millions of people who truly have it worse off than you do.

In contrast, what about these statements?

- "I learned today that my six-year-old son has stage 4 cancer."
- "My daughter committed suicide."
- "Three children are orphaned because both parents were killed in a car accident."

Those are examples of real-world problems that would be most people's worst nightmare come true. It is important to look at the contrast to bring perspective to what I am discussing (something I will elaborate on later).

Sheryl Sandberg, the chief operating officer of Facebook, gave a graduation commencement speech to the University of California, Berkley, class of 2016. During her speech, she opened up about how she was so incredibly devastated by her husband Dave's sudden death one year earlier. She explained how she was talking to a friend who was a psychologist and he suggested that she think about how things could have been worse. She said, "Are you kidding me? How could things be worse?"

He responded, "Dave could have had that same cardiac arrhythmia while he was driving your children."

She then said, "Wow. The moment he said it, I was overwhelmingly grateful that the rest of my family was alive and healthy. That gratitude overtook some of the grief."

Meriam-Webster Dictionary defines gratitude as "the state of being grateful; thankfulness." To put it simply, gratitude is taking the time to acknowledge all the things and people in our lives that are good and the ones that we appreciate. It is also recognizing that we are thankful for what we have so that we are able to shift our perspective from a negative one to a positive one.

If you happen to be someone who expresses themselves this way, it is completely okay! I did not write this book to point out everyone's flaws. I wrote this book so that you have the tools to recognize specific areas that are causing you periods of unhappiness.

Here's an example of what I am talking about with a negative statement: "I can't believe it took the waiter ten minutes to serve our drinks."

Instead, you can say this: "I am so grateful I am out with friends and we get to share each other's company."

If you slip and make a negative statement, as long as you catch yourself, you can finish it like this: "I can't believe it took the waiter ten minutes to serve our drinks. However, I am so grateful I am out with friends and we get to share each other's company."

This way, at least you caught yourself and still expressed your gratitude. Changing old patterns takes time. The key is recognizing how you are expressing yourself and making the effort to correct it. Please do not be hard on yourself, either! It has taken me years of practice to change my way of thinking. And trust me, I am still human and find myself complaining from time to time. It is completely okay! In fact, my husband will remind me when I am complaining, and I always joke and say, "I am not complaining, I am just explaining!" The difference is that I recognize it, call myself out, forgive myself, and express my gratitude.

Expressing gratitude is a way to shift your mood. I challenge you to list as many things that you are grateful for every day for the next thirty days. At first, if you can think of only one or two, that is perfect. I promise you if you do this every single day, you will be able to add things to your list. Make this list as soon as you awake each day, and keep a notebook next to your bed. It will feed your soul and get you off to a great start. I strongly urge you to handwrite the list every day and not type it or record it on your phone. Writing the list out by hand is very powerful, as it engages more of our senses. However, I do not want you to avoid making your gratitude list because it takes more effort to write it out by hand than to type it on your computer or phone. If all you can accomplish is to say them to yourself that is perfect too. There are also pages dedicated to your daily gratitude list at the end of this book.

If, at any point during your day, you find yourself feeling unhappy, angry, or negative, take a break and list as many things you can think of that you are grateful for. As you list each item, think about why you are grateful for it. Think about how it makes you feel, and take a minute to feel the gratitude. Repeat this over and over until your peace is restored and you feel better. The key is how it makes you feel. Gratitude is a high-energy word and causes our energy to shift to a positive state. Remember, the whole point is to shift your energy from negative to positive. Expressing gratitude is one way to achieve this.

Here is my (short) gratitude list for you to see as an example:

- my health, happiness, and spirituality
- my son

- my husband
- my family and friends
- my access to food, transportation, and shelter
- my ability to help others
- puppies, kittens, and elephants

I listed myself first because I have to always recognize that I need to take care of and be grateful for who I am so that I can take care of and be there for everyone else in my life. The order in which you list the people and things you are grateful for is irrelevant. I simply wanted to make a point about listing yourself first as a reminder and to reiterate that you are the most important person in your life.

Practice gratitude and feel its loving embrace. Life is too short not to experience this!

CHAPTER 9

SHIFTING PERSPECTIVE

Earlier, I mentioned changing your perspective, which can make or break your ability to experience happiness. So much of what I am discussing will ultimately lead to a shift in your perspective. Shifting your perspective, whether by forgiving someone or expressing gratitude for what you have, will help you see things in a different way. Your perception is merely how you perceive the world around you. It is kind of like wearing glasses. Your perception is like the lens that you are looking through.

I sometimes joke that one of my superpowers is the ability to see things in a different perspective. Basically, every situation I am in, I can see things from at least two different perspectives, sometimes more. Sometimes it is a blessing, and other times, it feels like a curse because I tend to be stubborn at times (although my husband and son would probably suggest that I am stubborn a lot). Shifting your perspective simply takes a bit of imagination.

Everyone has their own perception of the world in which they live. It is shaped by the way we were raised, the things we learn in school, influence from peers, and so on. Your perception may also change over time with the lessons we learn from our experiences. This perception that you have of the world is the lens through which you see the world, and in turn, you come to conclusions about things that take place.

The interesting thing about your perspective is that it is unique to you. My siblings and I each have a different perspective of our childhood, even though we were all raised by the same parents. The same is true for two employees working at the same company and reporting to the same supervisor. One may perceive that they have poor working conditions because they are asked to complete a project at the last minute, causing them to have to work late. The other employee, in the same situation, perceives it as an opportunity to shine and happily works late to complete the project. The good news is that at any point, you can shift your perspective.

I mentioned that I can sometimes be stubborn. This is because I always see things from multiple perspectives, and sometimes, I do not want to see it differently. Often, people do not want to shift their perspective because they feel it is part of their core belief system. While this way of thinking is perfectly okay, pay attention to the way the perspective makes you feel. Life is too short to hold on to a perspective that is causing you to feel unhappy.

The thing about your perspective is that it can end up becoming your reality. You see, your perspective is the lens through which you are looking. This will then become your perception of the situation. Your perception turns into your beliefs, which influences your behavior, which becomes your experience and ultimately your reality. My point here is if you change your perspective, you will change your reality.

Shift your perspective when you find yourself judging another person or situation. Again, there's always another way to look at the person or situation. Shift your perspective when you have negative thoughts; make it a positive thought instead. Shift your perspective when you are more concerned with what other people think of you. Remember, what other people think of you is none of your business! I hope I have made my point!

If you have not noticed, I like to use driving situations, as I experience so many on a daily basis. So here is another example: Someone cuts you off in traffic, and you automatically assume they did it deliberately. You could keep going about your day, holding onto the negative thought (resentment and anger) and being upset because of the jerk who almost hit you. If you have no desire to experience inner peace and happiness, that is perfect! However, if you want to be truly free when things like this happen, make up another story about what just occurred (shift your perspective).

Use your imagination, because you are never going to truly know what this person was thinking when they almost hit you. You also need to forgive them. Chances are they did not see you. You need to do whatever it takes to make that shift so you can release the anger and be free to carry on your day without holding on to unnecessary negative feelings. Life is too short to waste your thoughts on such petty things.

CHAPTER 10

....

MY STORY, PART 3: TRUST

Toward the end of 1999, my ex-husband and I started con-templating divorce. I had been told that I was never going to have children without medical assistance, and he and I were like oil and vinegar. We had been married for nine years, and I knew there was no way it would ever work out. Neither of us was happy in the relationship. We started marriage counseling and thought it would be a good idea to get away and have some fun together. I agreed to go on a vacation to Key West, Florida, along with my younger brother and his then-girlfriend (now my sister-in-law). The vacation was great, and after we returned and we fell back into our everyday routine, I still knew things were not going to work out between us. I was thirty-four years old and had my whole life ahead of me. I knew then that life was too short to be in an unhappy relationship.

On the day we agreed to separate, I dropped him off at the airport and went home. I realized that my period was ten days late and decided to take a home pregnancy test. I had been through this routine too many times to count, and every month, I always wondered whether or not I was pregnant. Per the norm, I carefully followed the directions of the home pregnancy test, and lo and behold, the test showed that I was pregnant! This was a complete miracle, as the fertility doctors told me that both of my fallopian tubes were 100 percent blocked and it would be next to impossible for me to conceive naturally.

This was also scary because I had been through this twice before only to be majorly disappointed. I immediately called the doctor because four months earlier, I had suffered an ectopic pregnancy and feared that this one could also be ectopic. The doctor had me come in and she performed an ultrasound. I was, in fact, pregnant and there was a healthy heartbeat. The doctor told me to gain weight and stop exercising because it was unclear if this would turn out to be a high-risk pregnancy.

When I called my soon to be ex-husband, he joked and said, "How does it feel to know you're going to be a single mother?" Needless to say, we continued in marriage counseling and decided to try to work things out. A healthy pregnancy seemed to be a sign from the Universe that it was not time for us to end our marriage.

This is where trust comes into the picture. Little did I know, trust would become a major theme for the next twenty years of my life and beyond. A friend of mine explained to me that during my pregnancy, all I could do was trust that everything was going to work out exactly how it is supposed to. Of course, I had to take good care of myself, and the rest was out of my control. This was very hard considering this was my third pregnancy. Eight and a half months and 70 pounds later, my miracle baby boy was born two weeks early.

I had no idea that when you have a baby, your ability to trust that things will work out the way they are supposed to is tested in unbelievable ways. All parents out there know exactly what I am talking about. Not a minute passes that you do not think about your children. All you can do is trust that they are going to be okay. You can control certain things with your children, while many other things are completely out of your control.

I ended up getting pregnant two more times and had two more miscarriages. After the last miscarriage, I decided I could not go through any more pain after having five pregnancies and one child. At that point, I was forty-one years old, and my son was almost seven. The thought of changing diapers again was exhausting. I could have had medical assistance to have another baby, and chose not to. I had a miracle child, after all! My marriage was always up and down, which also became exhausting for me.

After another ten years of marriage, from the time I learned I was pregnant with my son, I made the difficult decision to start the process of separating. For one year, we lived under the same roof, in separate bedrooms. I know he wanted to stay together for our son's best interest. However, I was not getting any younger, and I knew I deserved to be happy and in a relationship that was good for me. I moved out on my own in January 2011.

It was the most difficult thing I had ever done thus far in my life. It was like jumping off of a cliff and trusting that my wings worked. I knew that my life would be so much different than the life I had grown accustomed to in the previous twenty-plus years. I was now the single mother that I always knew I would be. I managed to make ends meet and had to start my career over after being out of the work force for close to ten years. It was a struggle, and life became much more difficult than I even realized it would be. I went back to college to finish my bachelor's degree, and I accomplished that in March of 2019. This was also extremely difficult managing a full-time job, college, and raising my son.

Fortunately, my ex-husband and I had an amicable divorce, and to this day, we remain close friends. Our focus is always on our son and his well-being, and we wanted to set a good example for him. I trusted that everything would work out, and it did—for a little while, anyway.

CHAPTER 11

TRUST, HAPPINESS, AND EXPECTATIONS

How do trust and happiness work hand in hand? It is actually quite simple. When you trust that things are going to work out exactly how they are supposed to, you can maintain a sense of peace around the situation. Some also refer to this as having faith—the belief or knowledge that things are going to work out. If you are constantly worrying about the outcome of a situation, that is insanity at its finest! Remember, if you can control a situation, stop worrying about it because you can control it. If you cannot control a situation, stop worrying about it because it is out of your control. Instead, practice trusting that the situation is going to be just fine. You may not know how it is going to work out; just know that it is. Will things always work out the way you think they should? Nope. It does not work that way. We do not always get everything we want.

This is where expectations come into the picture. When you trust that things are going to work out exactly how they are supposed to, you cannot attach any expectations to the situation. By attaching an expectation, you are trying to control the outcome. Let go of any expectation for things over which you have no control. By holding on to a specific expectation in a situation over which you have no control, you are setting yourself up for a major disappointment. So often do we fully trust that things are going to work out only to be disappointed. This is because we had some sort of expectation. If we did, in fact, fully trust that things would work out exactly how they were supposed to, there would be a level of peace around the situation.

This is also true when it comes to expecting people to behave in a specific way. Many disappointments stem from others failing to live up to our expectations of them when, in fact, they do not even know what we expect of them. How can you expect someone to behave in a specific way if they do not know what is expected of them? To me, this is Relationships 101. In all relationships, there must be communication, and we must never expect that the other person is going to do things that we would do or that we expect them to do. Instead, in all relationships, we must communicate our expectations.

If you start a new job, for example, how would you like it if your boss did not train you and simply expected you to know how to do the work? I do not think so! Even if you are a subject matter expert in any field, you would still need to know internal processes and so on. If a boss fails to train a new employee, they are setting that person up for failure. The same is true in any relationship. If I expect my son to call me on a specific day or time, I need to communicate that to him.

Never assume that the other person knows what you expect of them. When I was twenty years old and working as a legal secretary in Washington, DC, I had a boss that would regularly say to me, "When you assume, you make an ASS out of U and ME!" To this day, every time I hear the word "assume," I hear his voice saying that to me!

The next time you find yourself feeling disappointed

with another person, think about the communication that occurred and whether you may have set any expectations of them. Remember, people may not always behave the way you would. Life is too short to hold on to unrealistic expectations.

CHAPTER 12

MY STORY, PART 4: TRAGEDY STRIKES, YET AGAIN

It was 2013, and life was returning to normal after my divorce. I landed a really good job, which was putting me back on my desired career path. My son was thriving and had become accustomed to living life between two households, even though he really wished things were different, as most children of divorce will admit. I was dating my current husband, and we had begun planning our future together.

In the early morning hours on a Sunday in October, tragedy would strike my family again. I was at my boyfriend's house and woke up around 5:30 a.m., realizing I had left my phone in the kitchen. This bothered me because my son had spent the night at his friend's house, and I was worried that he had tried to reach me. I rushed down the stairs to retrieve my phone and was disturbed to see that I had a number of missed calls from my ex-husband. Minutes later, I kept getting these weird phone calls. When I answered, I heard a recording speaking Spanish. I do not speak any Spanish, so I immediately hung up each time, figuring it was a wrong number.

Later that morning, my ex-mother-in-law called me, as she was worried that she could not reach my ex-husband. I had a feeling that something bad had happened and did not want to tell her that. She would worry excessively, and I did not want to put her through any unnecessary angst. I told her he was probably still sleeping and that I would get back to her.

I called his then-girlfriend, and she said she could not discuss it with me. I told my ex-mother-in-law that I had learned that he was okay but I did not know exactly where he was. I tried to assure her that everything would be all right and I would call her the instant I found out what was going on. I became increasingly worried about what might have happened with my ex-husband, so I decided to leave my boyfriend's house and go pick up my son from his friend's house, to ensure he would detect nothing out of the ordinary. I had an overwhelmingly bad feeling that something awful had happened.

Around 2:00 p.m. that day, I received a call from my ex-husband. He sounded frantic. He told me what had happened and asked to speak to our son. My son was sitting on the sofa next to his friend when I handed him the phone. My son's reaction is one that will never escape my memory. After the call with his father, I remember seeing him on his hands and knees, crying and hitting the ground with both fists. It was heartbreaking to watch. This is how my son experienced the tragedy, as told in his college essay:

> The lessons we learn from obstacles we encounter can be fundamental to our future success. Recount a time when you faced a challenge, setback, or failure. How did it affect you and what did you learn from the experience? Growing up in Northern Virginia, it is a common theme for people to think that everything is handed to children and that they do not work for anything. I will admit I did have that until the 7th grade and I was not prepared for the one day that my life would change forever.

It was a Sunday. Being a diehard New York Giants fan, it was odd that I had not heard from him, as the game was only an hour away from kickoff. I looked at my phone to see how many times I called my father without an answer—15 calls. I started to worry and prepared myself for the worst, but nothing would prepare me for what I was about to hear. Suddenly, my mom ran into the room hysterical, tears falling down her face, and my life froze. I stood there, feeling nothing, almost as if I was empty inside.

I snapped back into reality and without a word she handed me the phone. It was my father. For a minute, I felt a sense of relief, but what followed the relief was a pain I would never wish on anyone. His voice was different and I could feel that something happened, something bad. He uttered the words '[Son], I messed up, I'm so sorry, I love you' and the phone cut off. The previous night my father was out at a bar, had a few drinks, and made the horrible decision to get behind the wheel. Because of that decision, two innocent people died. My father was everything to me. He helped me study and helped me grasp a better understanding of life.

The years that followed were a blur to me. I had fallen into the worst place I had ever been in and I was trapped inside of depression. Nothing mattered to me anymore. I always thought to myself, "Why me?" After the accident I was left hopeless, scared, and unmotivated. I continued to think this way all of 9th grade, until I met my best friend. She taught me that one mistake doesn't define a person and that I cannot let one moment ruin my life. She ultimately helped me to forget about all of my problems and motivated me to be independent and driven. Since the 9th grade, I have battled depression, anxiety, and ADD, but that has not stopped me from significantly increasing my GPA and overall becoming a better person.

My mother always says, "Everything happens for a reason", and I truly believe this because without the accident I would have been spoon fed my whole life. Because of the accident, I am independent and I make smarter choices. Most importantly, I learned that life happens in moments and that you cannot let one moment ruin the rest.

My son and I now live as if we have had two separate lives. We have "before the accident" and "after the accident." It was such a tragedy that affected so many people's lives. Two people were killed, an adult brother and sister lost their parents, and then there were my son and me. It was a situation no one is ever prepared to experience. The truly bizarre thing is that the accident happened just a few weeks after my son's thirteenth birthday, and I lost my brother two weeks before my thirteenth birthday. While I had experienced a traumatic tragedy at a tender young age, as my son had just experienced, they were different on so many levels. All I could do was be there for him, again trusting that everything would work out exactly the way it was supposed to. A year and two months after the accident, my ex-husband pled guilty without a trial and was sentenced to forty-one years in prison, with thirty-two years suspended.

My best friend, Dr. Sonja, reminded me that everything I had worked so hard to achieve—all the therapy sessions, coaching sessions, hundreds of books I read, and everything else I did to learn how to maintain a sense of peace and happiness—had prepared me for the hardest task at hand: raising a healthy and happy son who had just gone through something that few people, let alone children, are ever forced to deal with.

To this day, I will never know the sheer amount of pain, shame, and sense of loss that my son experiences daily. I remind him all the time that at least he still has his father and can visit him and talk to him on the phone. There are laws in place, and his father has to pay his debt to society. The children of the two people who lost their lives as a result of his father's mistake will never see their parents again. He understands this, and I am extremely proud of the young man he has become – how he overcame so many obstacles and is now a thriving college student.

I believe that every experience, whether good or bad, contains a lesson to be learned so you will grow and become a better person. With every disappointment, what can you learn from the experience? Sometimes, the lesson is in the experience itself. We are constantly being tested in life. Look at the disappointments you have experienced and see if you can figure out what you were meant to learn. Maybe there is no obvious reason or lesson—that's okay too. Keep trusting that everything works out for a reason, and when you learn the end result, the next step is to accept it.

CHAPTER 13

ACCEPTANCE

Acceptance is yet another practice that is much harder than it sounds. There are so many things that occur in life that we do not wish to accept. So many people dislike certain aspects about themselves. You may not like your straight hair and wish you had curly hair instead. You may not like the genetics you inherited from your parents, which make you prone to certain traits you wish you did not have. What can you do about it? Nothing. You have no choice but to accept it.

Remember earlier in the book, when I talked about my turned-up nose? I spent decades despising the way I looked, wishing I could change it. It was not until I went to a plastic surgeon and saw on a computer what my nose might look like that I finally came to terms with it and accepted it. It is really sad that I wasted so much of my life loathing how I looked. Life is too short to live like that!

So many people waste so much of their precious time wishing they had done things differently. Hey, I get it. There are so many things I wish I had done differently! Where can I start? I wish I finished college right after high school and experienced being in a sorority. I wish I had traveled with an ice show in my mid-twenties when I had the opportunity. I wish I didn't waste money on so many things I never use. I can go on and on.

My life has unfolded and continues to unfold exactly the way it is supposed to. I am the person I am today because of all the pain and joy I have experienced. If, at any point, I allow myself to go down the path of "I wish I had" or "If only I had," I stop myself right there and remind myself that if I had finished college right after high school, I probably would not have met my ex-husband and brought my son into this world. Everything has happened for a reason. If and when you go back into this vicious cycle, do not forget to forgive yourself. *Just do not beat yourself up.* Like everything I am discussing in this book, acceptance is no different. It takes time and a daily practice to make it a habit.

It took me years to accept what happened to my brother. While I will never fully understand why he was meant to die at such a young age, that tragedy transformed me into a self-help junkie, and can now pass on what I have learned to you and many other people. It has also made me a better person. Accept your past exactly as it is so you can be free to live in the present and experience being happy. Let the past go! Stop reliving it over and over. What is done is done.

In the introduction, I mentioned how we have to accept people for who they are and stop judging them for who they are not. When you judge another person, you are telling yourself they are not behaving in a way that you like or the way you *think* they should behave. You are making it about you—and it is about you. It is 100 percent your problem, and not the person whom you are judging. Instead, accept the person for who they are. You cannot change another person. All you can do is change the way you perceive them. If you are still struggling with that, please forgive yourself for judging them and work on acceptance. Maybe you need to work on forgiving them as well.

Here is an example: as a woman, I have experienced women judging other women a split second after meeting them. Many women will not even give another woman a chance. Because they are really thin and beautiful, they instantly do not like them. Talk about insanity at its finest! When you see someone and your perception is that they are more beautiful or thinner than you are, that is okay! You need to accept yourself *and* accept the beautiful woman you are likely admiring (and judging). Why can't you be happy for the beautiful, thin woman and stop making it about you?

I will reiterate that while you may perceive that she is more beautiful and thin than you are, you have no idea whatsoever what that woman has been through in her life. Most likely, she has had her own share of burdens to live with. Remember, you do not know what you do not know. Shift your perception instead to avoid going down that path. It is so much easier simply to accept the beautiful woman and move on with your life. Otherwise, you are wasting your precious moments and putting energy to something meaningless. Life is too short for that!

Here is something that I used to struggle with (and sometimes still do). I do not like to hear another person chewing their food. I do not know where this comes from. I just know that when I am sitting next to someone and I hear them chewing, it literally makes my skin crawl. In fact, it was something I used to get upset at my husband over. Then, one day, when he was eating his peanut butter and jelly sandwich with delight, I realized that I started to become increasingly irritated. It dawned on me that this was 100 percent my problem. I was allowing someone's natural tendency *to chew their food* irritate me. I had to laugh at myself. It was completely silly.

I began to really think about what I could do so that when I heard someone eating, it would not upset me. In the case of dealing with my husband, if I start to feel irritated, I remind myself that this is my problem, not his, and will either leave the room temporarily or turn the TV up louder. Sometimes I also take some deep breaths, which is a great way to relieve irritation and calm yourself down. (Take *ten* slow, deep breaths in through your nose and out your mouth.) In addition, this is something that I must accept so it does not disrupt my sense of peace.

There are many situations in daily life where acceptance needs to be practiced. Often, in order to accept something or someone, forgiveness is required before you are in a place where acceptance is even an option. If you are struggling with acceptance surrounding a particular person or situation, work on forgiveness first. It is hard to accept someone if you are still holding on to a resentment toward them.

Again, acceptance needs to be practiced with every opportunity that is presented to you. Sometimes, you have to work on acceptance over and over before it dissipates completely. That is okay, as long as you keep trying. Life is too short to hold on to the past.

CHAPTER 14

MIRACLES ARE ALL AROUND US!

You may be wondering why I am talking about miracles in a book about happiness. Miracles are shown to us in ways that help us keep *trusting* that everything is going to work out. It can be a sign that you see exactly when you need to see it. For some people, it is a specific number sequence that shows up frequently. Miracles or signs are the way the Universe connects with us to let us know that everything is going to work out exactly the way it is supposed to. However, you have to be open to seeing the signs that are constantly being presented to you.

While writing this book, I frequently asked the Universe to send me a sign to let me know I was on the right track with the information I am presenting you. In many ways, this has been a difficult yet therapeutic exercise for me, and at times I doubted myself. Without fail, I consistently saw the same sign. It was a specific animal, one you would not see unless you went to the zoo. I would see it online or on television, someone would refer to the animal in conversation, I had dreams about it, and so on. It held a significance to me, and every time I saw it, it confirmed I was doing what I was meant to do. It was comforting for me and kept me on track to continue working on this book.

I first discovered the idea that miracles were all around us in the mid-1990s. I was curious about what that looked like, and for days, I asked the Universe to show me a miracle. A few weeks went by, and nothing happened. I wanted so badly to experience something so I better understood what it meant to see a miracle unfold right in front of me.

Then, one day, I was driving home, and I stopped at a red light. I used to be a cigarette smoker and had recently quit. That day, I had an intense desire to buy a pack of cigarettes. For anyone who has been addicted to nicotine, you know exactly what I am talking about. It is immensely powerful and very difficult to maintain your willpower. I asked the Universe to help me stay strong. At that moment, I looked to my left and saw a beautiful young woman sitting in a convertible with the top down, and I saw the rays of sunlight reflecting off of her blond hair. I looked to the right and saw a frail old woman, with a wrinkled face, holding a cigarette in her hand, which was shaking uncontrollably. I watched her take a puff and slowly release the smoke. I wanted a smoke so badly. At that moment, as if on cue, my favorite Tom Petty song started to play on the radio:

> Well I won't back down,
> No I won't back down.
> You can stand me up at the gates of hell,
> But I won't back down.
> No I'll stand my ground.
> Won't be turned around.

Tears starting rolling down my face, and then I started laughing from deep within my belly—the best kind! That was a miracle. That was the Universe supporting my request to help me so I would not start smoking again. It was subtle yet very powerful, especially when the song started playing. For me, music resonates deep within me in ways many people do not experience. It also demonstrated a sense of humor in way that I could relate to: a beautiful young woman or an old frail woman whose life would be cut short, likely due to smoking.

My son was also given a profound miracle in April 2019. He called me one afternoon and was crying. Being the momma bear that I am, I started almost screaming, "Oh no, what's wrong?" As he described the encounter, I too could not hold back the tears:

"Me and my friend went to get some food at a burger joint. I saw an Italian sub shop next door and decided to get my food there instead. I walked in, ordered my sub, and went back to the burger joint, where my friend was and sat down and ate with him. We finished eating and started walking toward our cars. When I got close to my car, a man approached us. He asked me if I had been in the sub shop earlier. I said yes, I was. Then he said, 'My name is Nathan, and I have a very close relationship with God, and as soon as you walked in, God told me to let you know that he knows that today is a very difficult day for you and wants you to know that everything is going to be okay. He also asked me to remind you that he is with you at all times and that I should take more time to ask for assistance and guidance.' The man turned around, walked to his car, and drove away."

The first words out of my mouth were, "That was not just a miracle. The Universe sent you a messenger." What the stranger could not have possibly known was why that day was a very difficult one for my son. That day was his father's birthday. Special days like birthdays, Thanksgiving, and Christmas are especially hard for my son since his father is away. What I found interesting about this particular incident is that my son's friend witnessed the miracle as well. The next day, I saw his friend, and we briefly talked about it. His friend started tearing up as well. It was truly a beautiful experience for my son and his friend that they will never forget.

There is another type of miracle that I experienced three times in my life before the age of nineteen. In fact, it is a miracle that I am still alive. Because of the three accidents I was involved in, I have always felt that I have a guardian angel.

The first accident was when I was around the age of three, when we were living in Baltimore, Maryland. I do not remember the accident because I was too young, so I have to rely on the story I was told from my mother and my siblings. Apparently, my sister and two brothers walked across the street to a field to free a turtle they had found. I decided to follow them and ran into the street right in front of a car. My father and his best friend were outside and they realized that the driver's side front tire was sitting on my shoulder. The car needed to be lifted off of me. Fortunately, a fire station was close by, and the firemen witnessed the accident and came running over to help lift the car off of me. My father carefully pulled me out from under the car. I was unconscious. My mother ran into the house crying, as she thought I was seriously injured or, worse, dead. I regained consciousness and was taken to the hospital. Miraculously, I only suffered multiple cuts and bruises on my back. I vaguely remember my father changing the bandages multiple times a day.

The second accident happened in the early-morning hours on New Year's Day when I was sixteen years old. I was at a party with a friend of mine, and I was supposed to be staying at her house overnight. Sometime after midnight, I could not find her. At this point, I was already way past my curfew and was afraid to go home, as my father was very strict when it came to this. I talked to another friend of mine, and she said I could stay at her house.

We got dropped off at her house around 2:00 a.m., and I was preparing to sleep on the floor in her room. She then told me that she took the keys to her parents' car and wanted to go back to the party. I told her I thought that was a really bad idea and I did not want any part of it. She insisted I go with her, so I did. We stayed at the party until around 5:00 a.m.

On the way back to her house, we were driving on a winding road. I was falling in and out of sleep, and my head was leaning on the passenger window. I remember hearing her say that two of her relatives had had car accidents on that same road. Then I fell back asleep. Suddenly, the car started to lose control. I opened my eyes and saw the car racing head-on into a large tree. I put my arms out in front of me to brace myself for the collision and watched in what seemed like slow motion as the car pounded into the tree. This was long before seatbelts and airbags were commonplace. My friend's face smashed into the windshield. Miraculously, I was not thrown through the windshield, as I had nothing to stop me.

Another car from the party happened to be following behind us and was able to get to a phone to call 911. This was also before cell phones were invented. The paramedics arrived and began caring for my friend. They asked me how I was and determined I was okay. They took her to the hospital, where she received more than one hundred stitches. The people in the car behind us took me back to the party. At this point, I just wanted to go home.

I eventually found someone I knew who gave me a ride home. I had bumps in multiple places on my head, and when I took my winter coat off, there were cuts all over my back. I have no idea how they got there because my coat was not damaged at all. Both my hands and arms were so badly bruised from absorbing the impact that I could not use them for days. It was a miracle that we both survived, and I was incredibly grateful we were alive.

My third accident, and hopefully the last, happened when I was eighteen. My family had moved to Milford, Delaware, and I went camping with some high school friends near Ocean City, Maryland, which was roughly an hour away from my home. The next morning, I got up and decided to drive home early, as the weather was not going to be very good that particular Sunday. It was just starting to rain, and the roads were likely slick. I looked away momentarily to either change the radio station or put out a cigarette in the car's ashtray. When I looked back up, there was a turn in the road I was not expecting. I lost control of the car, and it rolled several times, going off the road and into a field. Again, I was not wearing a seatbelt, and there was no airbag. The driver's side window was fully down. It was a miracle that I was not thrown out of the car.

The car stopped rolling and was still on its side. I stood up and could barely open the car door, as it was extremely heavy when trying to push it up. I saw a bunch of people outside a church located across the street, and about five men were running toward me. They managed to pull me out of the car and turn it back upright. It was drivable, although one of the tires was flat. One of the men changed the tire for me, and I was able to drive home. I did not have any injuries whatsoever. After replacing multiple tires, I learned that the frame was bent on the car and I needed to replace the car entirely. Again, I was just grateful to be alive.

Miracles are all around us, all the time. Pay attention to the world around you, and try to be open to witnessing them. Ask the Universe to show you one, and trust that it will be presented exactly when it is meant to be. Trust me, life is too short to live without miracles!

CHAPTER 15

RANDOM ACTS OF KINDNESS

Kindness is such an important part of happiness because there is nothing that can make you feel better than to help someone out who is not expecting you to. It is also called "paying it forward." One very simple way to do this is when you are passing people by, look them in the eye, smile, and say hello. You do not know what you do not know, and maybe that simple smile from a stranger will help someone who is going through something awful feel better. It is another random act of kindness.

After my son was born, I began to see people differently. When I witnessed someone being mean or just simply being a jerk, I would think about the fact that that person started out as an innocent baby. I would think about what must have happened to them to learn that behavior. You see, we all start out as innocent babies. Then the world gets to us, and we forget the innocence we once had as a child. So, the next time you see someone being mean or a jerk, remember that they used to be an innocent baby and try not to judge them. Instead, forgive them and give them a smile.

A long time ago, I was driving down a busy highway and went through a toll booth. It gets congested leaving that toll booth because everyone has to merge from four lanes into three. They are not marked very well, so it can be tricky. That day, I witnessed some road rage right in front of me. A woman was trying to merge, and another car was probably driving too fast for the area and for the number of cars that were trying to merge. She merged into the lane, and the other driver became furious, as she appeared to have cut him off. Perhaps he could have slowed down and let her in, and instead, he chose to be angry.

He proceeded to drive right next to her and repeatedly made it look like he was going to hit her by sharply turning his car close to hers. I could see him yelling, sticking his middle finger up, and then he made a gun with his fingers and began mimicking shooting her. It was such a horrific act of road rage that had me shaking.

I feel compelled now to ask: If you are one of those people who behave this way would you treat someone that way if you were face to face with them and they accidently walked into you? Would you scream profanities and threaten to hit or kill them? Probably not!

Anyway, a minute later, I passed the woman in the car and looked over at her. She was visibly upset. Even though we were driving, I tried to let her know that it was okay and that it was not her fault and I was sorry she had to go through this. She waved at me, and I went about my day. A few days later, I received an email from the woman thanking me for my act of kindness. She explained that she was having such a horrible day, and my display of compassion for her helped her tremendously. I wrote her back letting her know that I had been in her shoes many times and wanted to let her know it was not about her. That man had anger issues and was taking it out on her. I was actually more curious as to how she got my email address. She replied, "Your license plate."

This was after my novel was published in 2009. The main theme in the book was "4give4peace." My license plate read "4gve4pc." I also had a nonprofit that I founded with the same name. She did an internet search using the phrase, and it led her right to me. It was a humbling experience knowing that I was able to help a stranger have a better day.

Here is another heartwarming story about a random act of kindness that my cousin Grace experienced:

"God's timing is always perfect. Tonight, I was driving one of the babies I was watching home. I am in the middle of the city when my car shuts off in an extremely busy spot. Possibly one of the worst parts in the city. I tried more than twenty times to restart my car, and it was not working. I called the parents of the baby and Geico to come. While I am waiting and still continuing to try to start my car multiple times, this lady walks up and says, 'Honey, do you need help?' At that point, I tell her I called Geico and the parents but couldn't get out of the car because of the baby. Mind you, at this time, I have been cussed at multiple times and honked at by cars trying to get by. The lady says, 'It is okay, dear. I'll direct traffic.' I try to start my car several more times.

"Then a man walks over who knew the lady, and he says 'We are getting cables to jump start your car but try to start it so I can listen to the sound it is making and see if I can figure out what it is.' I then try to start the car. After more than fifty attempts, it starts! He then asks me to turn it off and on a couple of times. I kid you not—every time it started right back up. The lady and the man then proceeded to get in their car so they could follow me to the baby's house and then to my home, which is twenty-five minutes away.

"The last thing the lady asks me is 'What's your name?'

"I say, 'Grace.'

"She says, 'We were meant to meet tonight!' Some call it coincidence. I call it God! It gave me chills."

Throughout the course of every day, please notice the opportunities to practice random acts of kindness. It will warm your heart and soul, and you will be rewarded in ways you may never know. Life is too short to *not* pay it forward.

CHAPTER 16

WALK THROUGH THE PAIN

When life happens (while you are busy making other plans), how are you going to handle it? The information I am sharing with you contains things you can do every single day of your life. None of this information is meant to be shared to trivialize tragedy, loss, or situations that cause you intense pain or anger. When you experience a loss, whether it be a loved one, friend, marriage, or job, or any other situation that causes you deep pain or anger, do whatever you need to do to take the time to feel the pain. Grieve, cry, and experience all the emotions you are feeling. They are real and are meant to be felt. You must go through the sadness before you can get to the other side and forgive, trust, accept, and shift your perspective.

I remind you of this because I have been through so much pain in my life, and I did not take care of myself and do what I needed to do to feel the pain. I know how miserable it feels. I tried everything I could to avoid it. You can walk over it, around it, under it, and it remains, and it will come back to haunt you when you least expect it. I do not want that for you. Walk through the pain and experience every bit of it. Seek the help of a therapist, your friends and family, or a support group – whatever feels right for you so you can get to a place where you are able to shift your perspective and live the life that you deserve.

Years ago, we were on vacation and were having dinner with another family. We were at a pizzeria, and I was sitting next to a bright eight-year-old girl. I cannot remember exactly what we were talking about, and I will never forget what she said. It was the type of simple brilliance that you sometimes hear from children. She said, "Sometimes you have to go through the bad stuff to get to the good stuff."

When you are experiencing pain from a situation in your life for the first time, it can feel like the worst possible thing that could ever happen to you or anyone else. If it is the first time you have experienced such deep pain, then it absolutely is! Pain is pain, regardless of the situation that caused it.

I am an animal lover and for the most part I have always had a pet ever since I can remember. My first pet as an adult was a cat named Chelsea. I loved her so much! However, she had a love-hate relationship with humans. She grew to be fourteen pounds which was overweight for a small cat. At the age of thirteen, she began to rapidly lose weight. The veterinarian alluded that she likely had cancer and I made the most difficult decision of my life to have her euthanized. I left the veterinary hospital in hysterics. It was a pain I had never experienced.

A few years later, my ten year old border collie, Nelson, began to slowly deteriorate and I had to make the decision to have him euthanized. Because I had been through this once before, I thought I would be able to handle it and be stronger. Once again, I left the veterinary hospital in hysterics. I remember this time it seemed even worse than my previous experience with Chelsea. What I learned is that when we experience any type of pain, it does not get easier. I do believe I was stronger as a result, yet the pain was still raw and debilitating.

There are so many levels of pain that we humans experience. And again, I am in no way trivializing anyone's experiences as there are so many things I hope to never have to endure. When you experience any type of pain, walk through it and take the time to grieve and be gentle with yourself. You will awaken a stronger person as a result. Life is too short to suffer and struggle with the pain.

CHAPTER 17

TIME TO BE HAPPY

As I have said many times, being happy is not always easy, and it may not come naturally. The world we live in today is chaotic, and more often than not, it feels crazy. There are mass shootings regularly. The political arena is a mess. There are more natural disasters today than most can re-member. More and more people are getting sick. All these things can and will affect your ability to maintain your sense of peace.

I urge you to take the time to go through the daily exer-cises that follow. All these things need to be practiced, and none of them will be mastered:

- First, focus on the areas in your life where you are ex-periencing stress and identify any areas in which you are causing your own unhappiness.
- Work on taking care of yourself and figure out what you can do to find your passion and purpose in life.
- Practice forgiving others and, most importantly, for-giving yourself.
- Make a gratitude list every single day for thirty straight days, and remember, if at any time during the day you need to make a shift, make another gratitude list.

- Pay attention to your thoughts and shift your perspective when needed.
- Trust that everything is going to work out exactly the way it is supposed to.
- Are there any situations in which you have placed any unreasonable expectations?
- What are the areas in your life where you need to focus on acceptance?
- Stay open to experiencing all the miracles that are being presented to you every single day.
- Practice random acts of kindness!
- Walk through the pain.

The joy I felt when I was climbing the one hundred steps from our river dock to my house as a child were the happiest moments I remember. My life has become a journey of learning how to get back to that feeling. I live my life always looking up, moving forward, and striving to maintain my sense of peace and happiness. Climbing one hundred steps can be hard at first and the same is true when learning to be happy. It takes discipline and determination to create lasting change, one step at a time and one day at a time.

So what I hope for you, my friend, is that you take to heart the information I have provided and do the work. Build a good relationship with the most important person in your life—you. Relationships take work, and having a good one with yourself is no different. I hope that you embrace and respect yourself enough to practice self-forgiveness so you can truly experience self-love, accept your beautiful self just the way you are, and trust that everything is going to work out exactly as it should. Pay attention to all the miracles being presented around you. Stay open to seeing and experiencing them. Practice random acts of kindness and pay it forward. You will be rewarded!

There is no guarantee how long you have left. Your life will pass you by in a split second, as will those of everyone with whom you love. How do you want to spend each and every day while you are still here? Life is too short to delay the climb!

EXERCISES

Throughout *Happiness Solved*, I discuss exercises you can do to bring to your attention to things you may be doing or thinking that affect your ability to feel peace and happiness. For the next thirty days, I challenge you to do these exercises. By doing these for thirty straight days, you will begin to create a habit so that you can create lasting change. There may be days when you may not experience all of them, so focus on areas that need your attention. The only exception is the gratitude list. I highly recommend you complete this list each morning before you start your day, and any time during the day when you need to shift your perspective.

STRESSORS

Stress is a major factor that can affect your ability to remain peaceful and happy. What are some areas in your life where stress is affecting you? In the space below or in a notebook, list all the stressors you are experiencing. Next to them, list all the ways that you can alleviate or eliminate the stressors in your life.

Stressor   How the stressor can be alleviated or eliminated?

....

....

....

....

....

....

....

....

....

....

....

....

NEGATIVITY

Having a negative attitude or even thinking negative thoughts regularly is going to lower your energy levels. Are there any areas in your life where you are feeling negativity? Below, list any of the negative thoughts that you think regularly. Next to them, list replacement thoughts that can help you shift the thought to a more positive one.

Negative Thought   Replacement Thought

·································   ·································

·································   ·································

·································   ·································

·································   ·································

·································   ·································

·································   ·································

·································   ·································

·································   ·································

·································   ·································

·································   ·································

·································   ·································

·································   ·································

WHAT IS YOUR STORY?

You create a story when you make an assumption of what you believe is going to happen or what you believe has just occurred. It is simply creating a drama in your mind without any facts on which to base it on.

Think about a situation where you have created a story. Pay attention to how it makes you feel and if there are any festering negative emotions. List all the stories you have made up. Next to each one, create a new story around the situation. Read the new story to yourself several times. Now pay attention to how the new story resonates within you.

Your Story   New Story

....

....

....

....

....

....

....

....

....

CRITICIZING YOURSELF

Criticizing yourself is a common practice for many people. In what ways have you criticized yourself? In the space below or in a notebook, list the critical/negative thought on one side, and on the other side, list a positive thought to replace the negative one. For example, a negative thought could be "I am so overweight." A positive replacement thought could be "My body is beautiful, and I accept and love myself exactly the way I am."

Negative Thought   Positive Thought

....

....

....

....

....

....

....

....

....

....

WORRYING ABOUT WHAT OTHER PEOPLE THINK OF YOU

"What other people think of you is none of your business." How many times a day are you consciously thinking about what other people think of you? Are you even aware of it?

Write down the things that you generally worry about what other people think of you. Maybe you are subconscious about your weight, or maybe you worry about people liking you. The next step here is to forgive yourself and work on acceptance.

Below, list all the things you worry about what other people think of you.

....

....

....

....

....

....

....

....

....

CRITICIZING AND JUDGING OTHERS

What are some thoughts or statements you have expressed about others? In the space below or in a notebook, list the critical/judgmental thought about a person on one side. On the other side, replace it with a positive thought about the person. For example, a critical thought of another person could be "That dress makes her look heavy." Instead, change your thought to "She looks perfect in that dress."

Critical/Judgmental Thought   Positive Thought

....

....

....

....

....

....

....

....

....

....

CONTROL OR NO CONTROL

If you cannot control it, do not worry about it because you cannot control it. If you can control it, do not worry about it because you can control it.

What are things you worry about that you can control? What are the things you worry about that you cannot control? What do you worry about the most? In the space below, list the things you worry about the most. In the space next to it, answer yes or no whether you can control it. In the last column, list the action you can take or if it is simply something that you have to trust. For example, you may worry about getting sick. Can you control it? Yes and no. What you can do about it is control how you take care of yourself by eating healthily and exercising. Then all you can do is trust that you will remain healthy.

What do I worry about the most?	Can I control it?	What can I do about it?
....	....	....
....	....	....
....	....	....
....	....	....
....	....	....
....	....	....
....	....	....

JEALOUSY

Any feelings of jealousy are going to eat you up inside in ways you cannot even imagine. List any jealous thoughts about someone or something. The next step is to forgive yourself and shift your perspective toward the person or situation. Remember, that same person you may feel jealous about has parts of them you would never want for yourself.

Below, list any feelings of jealousy you have experienced.

....

....

....

....

....

....

....

....

....

....

BE YOURSELF

The next time you are about to do something that may be out of your comfort zone, do a gut check. How does it feel? Is it something that you will truly enjoy, or are you doing it to be seen by others or feel like you fit in? If you recognize something that you are doing or have done that is not who you want to be or do, list it below. The next step is to forgive yourself so you can love yourself enough to be who you want to be and do what you want to do.

List below the things you have done where you are not being true to yourself.

. . . .

. . . .

. . . .

. . . .

. . . .

. . . .

. . . .

. . . .

. . . .

WHAT ARE YOU PASSIONATE ABOUT?

Everyone needs something that they are passionate about—something that gives their life more purpose. In the space below or in notebook, make a list of everything that interests you:

....

....

....

....

....

....

....

....

....

....

....

....

....

TAKING CARE OF *YOU!*

Make a list of things you can do to make you feel good. These are things you may not do regularly.

....

....

....

....

....

....

....

....

....

....

....

....

....

FORGIVING OTHERS

Check in with yourself and think of a person who did something that upset or hurt you. If you are feeling anything but love for this person, you may still be holding onto resentment. Make a list of people you need to forgive. Once you have identified each person, either say it to yourself or write it down as follows: "I forgive _____ for _____." Remember, you may have to repeat this every day or anytime that person enters your thoughts and brings up the negative feelings associated with what they did.

People I need to forgive:

. . . .

. . . .

. . . .

. . . .

. . . .

. . . .

. . . .

. . . .

. . . .

FORGIVING YOURSELF

What are things that you have done to others in which you need to forgive yourself? What are things you have done to yourself? Make a list of all the ways you need to forgive yourself. Next, say to yourself or write it down as follows: "I forgive myself for _____." Repeat this as many times as needed to feel a sense of peace toward yourself and promote self-love.

I need to forgive myself for:

. . . .

. . . .

. . . .

. . . .

. . . .

. . . .

. . . .

. . . .

. . . .

GRATITUDE LIST

For the next thirty days, in the space below or in a notebook, make a list of everything you have to be grateful for in your life. Pay attention to how you feel when you write down each word.

....

....

....

....

....

....

....

....

....

....

....

....

DAY 1:

....

....

....

....

....

....

....

....

....

....

....

....

....

....

DAY 2:

....
....
....
....
....
....
....
....
....
....
....
....
....
....

DAY 3:

....

....

....

....

....

....

....

....

....

....

....

....

....

....

DAY 4:

....

....

....

....

....

....

....

....

....

....

....

....

....

....

....

DAY 5:

....

....

....

....

....

....

....

....

....

....

....

....

....

....

DAY 6:

....
....
....
....
....
....
....
....
....
....
....
....
....
....

DAY 7:

....

....

....

....

....

....

....

....

....

....

....

....

....

....

DAY 8:

....
....
....
....
....
....
....
....
....
....
....
....
....
....

DAY 9:

....

....

....

....

....

....

....

....

....

....

....

....

....

....

DAY 10:

....

....

....

....

....

....

....

....

....

....

....

....

....

....

....

DAY 11:

....

....

....

....

....

....

....

....

....

....

....

....

....

....

DAY 12:

....
....
....
....
....
....
....
....
....
....
....
....
....
....
....

DAY 13:

....

....

....

....

....

....

....

....

....

....

....

....

....

....

DAY 14:

....
....
....
....
....
....
....
....
....
....
....
....
....
....

DAY 15:

....

....

....

....

....

....

....

....

....

....

....

....

....

....

DAY 16:

....
....
....
....
....
....
....
....
....
....
....
....
....
....

DAY 17:

....
....
....
....
....
....
....
....
....
....
....
....
....
....

DAY 18:

....

....

....

....

....

....

....

....

....

....

....

....

....

....

DAY 19:

....
....
....
....
....
....
....
....
....
....
....
....
....
....

DAY 20:

....
....
....
....
....
....
....
....
....
....
....
....
....

DAY 21:

....

....

....

....

....

....

....

....

....

....

....

....

....

....

DAY 22:

....

....

....

....

....

....

....

....

....

....

....

....

....

....

DAY 23:

....

....

....

....

....

....

....

....

....

....

....

....

....

....

DAY 24:

....

....

....

....

....

....

....

....

....

....

....

....

....

....

DAY 25:

....

....

....

....

....

....

....

....

....

....

....

....

....

....

DAY 26:

....
....
....
....
....
....
....
....
....
....
....
....
....
....

DAY 27:

....
....
....
....
....
....
....
....
....
....
....
....
....
....

DAY 28:

....
....
....
....
....
....
....
....
....
....
....
....
....
....

DAY 29:

....

....

....

....

....

....

....

....

....

....

....

....

....

....

DAY 30:

....

....

....

....

....

....

....

....

....

....

....

....

....

....

DISAPPOINTMENTS

Make a list of any situation where you have experienced a disappointment. What can you learn from it? Pay attention to the expectation you had concerning the situation. Is forgiveness needed?

Disappointment	What can be learned, and was there an expectation?
. . . .	. . . .
. . . .	. . . .
. . . .	. . . .
. . . .	. . . .
. . . .	. . . .
. . . .	. . . .
. . . .	. . . .
. . . .	. . . .
. . . .	. . . .
. . . .	. . . .
. . . .	. . . .
. . . .	. . . .

ACCEPTANCE

Below or in a separate notebook, list the things you noticed throughout the day where you need to practice acceptance. If there is someone in your life who exhibits a particular behavior that you dislike, you likely need to accept this person exactly the way they are. Remember, you cannot change them. You can only change your perception of that person. Do you need to forgive them as well? Remember, sometimes forgiveness is needed before acceptance is an option.

....

....

....

....

....

....

....

....

....

....

ABOUT THE AUTHOR

Sandee Sgarlata earned a bachelor's degree in business. She is an author, certified life coach, public speaker, retired US national and international figure skating coach, and has worked twenty years helping people create lasting changes in their lives. Because of tragedies that affected her, she has spent the last thirty years in her own quest to find and maintain a sense of peace and happiness. Sgarlata lives in Northern Virginia with her husband and son.

www.SandeeSgarlata.com